Breaking
the Cycle of
Child Abuse

Breaking the Cycle of Child Abuse

by Christine
Comstock Herbruck

Winston Press

Library of Congress Catalog Card Number: 78-59405
ISBN (paper): 0-03-045691-6
ISBN (cloth): 0-03-052691-4
Printed in the United States of America

5   4   3   2   1

Winston Press, Inc.
430 Oak Grove
Minneapolis, MN 55403

To my small family—Peter, Jonathan, Katy, and Tommy—

and to my large family—Mary, Wendy, Ruth, Lil, Vicki, Jean, Anna, Kandy, Rosemary, Jody, and Kathy—

this book is dedicated with love.

Acknowledgments

Thanks to all of you whose stories appear within these pages. Your willingness to share your pain and your love will surely enrich other lives as it has enriched mine.

Thanks to Gerda Freedheim for your strength and your direction.

Thanks to Bee Page for encouraging me to write.

Thanks to the George Gund Foundation for making the work of Parents Anonymous of Northeastern Ohio possible.

Thanks to Don Freedheim for your help in formulating the definition of child abuse for this book.

Thanks to Steve Hopewell for your constant enthusiastic support and for keeping Parents Anonymous of Northeastern Ohio stable as I finished this book.

Thanks to Dee Ready for your considerate and thoughtful editing but especially for your sensitive and loving self.

Thanks to Leonard Lieber for beginning Parents Anonymous and for staying with it as it has grown.

Thanks to Michael Schachere for your portrayal of Yvette and Paul in Chapter 10 and for your creative challenges.

Thanks to Mary for adding immeasurably to my understanding of the cycle of child abuse, our group, and my life.

Table of Contents

Preface

No one is more opposed to child abuse than the people who know it best, the people who were abused themselves as children and who are now abusing their own children. They know what abuse is like. They're the "experts." They know the feelings that lead up to and explode during an abusive episode. They know how the past burdens the present. They know that the future looms relentlessly bleak unless they get help.

This book contains the stories of a number of people who abused their children and who finally, in desperation, called a group known as Parents Anonymous for help. The stories of their cry for help and the answers which came will be helpful, we believe, to other people who are having trouble with abuse or who are aware of others who need help. This is a book for people who care about others.

Parents Anonymous is a self-help group for parents* who have abused or who fear they might abuse their children. These parents meet together weekly with a sponsor who acts as a facilitator, work together to discover how not to abuse their children, and support each other in times of crisis to prevent abuse.

Parents Anonymous members form family-type relationships within their groups. For most PA people, their group is the first good family experience they have had. PA is a safe place to experiment with untried ways of behaving and new styles of relating; things learned in the PA group can be taken home and used in the actual family environment.

In addition, the group provides a crisis telephone contact for its members. They learn to call one another for help rather than to take out their frustrations and anger on their children. They learn to give help as well as to receive it. The PA group provides an opportunity for members to share insights and discoveries so that they can learn to predict high risk times and ward them off. Parents learn to defuse situations, either emotionally or physically, *before* they lose control, or they learn to do something other than abuse a child when they *do* lose control.

I count myself lucky to be associated with the Parents Anonymous members I've known and to have the opportunity to share with you their stories and my own story as a Parents Anonymous sponsor.

*The word *parent* is used here to refer to any person in a position of major responsibility or authority over a child. Thus, a parent may be a mother, a father, a boyfriend, a stepmother, an aunt, or anyone else who parents a child.

I had been the co-founder of a small group-dynamics organization in Cleveland and my occupation was leading groups. In addition, the prevention of child abuse had been a major interest of mine for several years. In 1974, I was instrumental in initiating a program at a Cleveland hospital to help abused children and their parents.

Yet, when I was asked in March of 1976 to sponsor a PA group, I hesitated. I had never heard of Parents Anonymous, and I certainly didn't have any free time. The person who contacted me was very persuasive, however, and insisted that Parents Anonymous worked. It sounded like a challenge, so I agreed to sponsor a group.

With Gerda Freedheim, Ray Bowen, Clara Simmons, and myself, Parents Anonymous was born in Cleveland. Today there are fifteen chapters in that city, and I presently coordinate and administer the Cleveland program. In the beginning, whatever free time I had was quickly spoken for. I did some of the coordinating, some of the public speaking, some of the orientation activities, and all of the telephoning. Like any new idea, Parents Anonymous struggled at first. It took time to become known and time to catch on.

For example, early in the program we publicized a telephone number which parents could call when they felt they needed help. But our number was only slowly recognized and accepted by abusive parents. We received one call a week or so, and then slowly the calls increased—first to a few a week, then to one almost every day, then to one a day, and finally to several each day. Not all the callers are parents, but most of them are. Not all the calls are about physical abuse—in fact, the majority are not—but every call is about abuse of one kind or another. Some of the parents who do call in are going through serious crisis times in their lives; others are simply at the point where they're ready to work on their abuse problem. Over the past two and a half years, I have personally spoken to three hundred fifty parents who have serious reason to fear child abuse. I have learned a great deal from these calls.

It has been in my experiences with my own Parents Anonymous group that I have learned the most intimate aspects of child abuse. In this book, you will meet my teachers and my friends. You will meet Mary** who called long distance to California to find out about Parents Anonymous, then became, as she puts it, a "crisis pen pal" because there was no one close to

** Throughout this book, pseudonyms are used for the names of all parents who have called Parents Anonymous or joined the Cleveland chapter.

her in Cleveland. It was not until four years later that she met her crisis pen pal face to face. By then, she had already heard about and joined a Cleveland Parents Anonymous group. Mary's husband now belongs to Parents Anonymous, too, and there haven't been any objects thrown through their living room wall in a long time.

Lil's enthusiasm about breaking her cycle of child abuse, which is talked about in this book, has stayed with her even during those times when she thought she'd fail. You're bound to like Lil, along with Vicki and her angry little boys—Vicki, whose laugh was the loudest and whose tears were the sorriest; Vicki who now handles her life, her children, and her home as quietly and competently as anyone could ever dream.

Carole, Jean, and Kathy are sisters. They share a background, a family, and a life today. Knowing little about good parenting, little about positive living in general, these three, together with the help of PA, are restructuring their own families. Their mother watches with amazement, anger, and sorrow as Kathy appears on TV, telling of her change from a seventeen-year-old alcoholic to a good mother. Kathy knows about alcoholics; her father was one, too. That enables her to understand others who are facing the same problems.

I have been intimately involved in the lives of eleven people for two years now. I have been with them alone and in group meetings; I have talked with their therapists, their children, their mates, their parents, and their friends. I have been with them as they faced death and as they gave birth. I have been with them in tears and in laughter. I have come to know and to love the people in this PA group, and I join with them to offer these stories to you. I am deeply grateful to each one of them for sharing first with me and now with you something of themselves. I am also grateful to them for the understanding and the patience they showed to me as I wrote this book.

Section I
THE PROBLEM

Chapter 1
A Cry for Help

A phone call born out of fear, desperation, and love can be one of the first steps in breaking the cycle of child abuse. A phone call like the one from Barb, a young woman who was abused as a child, a woman in great need in an overwhelmingly stressful time in her life, can be a new beginning. When I answered Barb's call, I heard the sharp, terrified scream of a baby in pain and Barb's low moaning agony. The sounds of their keening made a tragic chorus at the other end of the telephone.

"I've killed my baby. I've finally done it; I'm so bad. I should be killed; I've killed Ali."

"Hold on, Barb, we can handle this," I assured her. "You're not alone anymore, remember? You have help. We can handle this. I'm glad you've called."

"I've killed my baby, my sweet, little baby, my only baby. I love her so much, and I killed her," Barb continued to moan.

"Barb, you haven't killed your baby. I can hear her crying."

"I've killed my baby," she insisted, "and I love her so much!"

"Barb, listen to me. You have NOT killed your baby. She's yelling her head off. She isn't dead, but she needs your help. Barb, you have to help her now. She needs you to be calm. How does she look?"

"I should be killed, how could I hurt that darling little baby? She's my best friend. She's the only one in the world who loves me. How could I hurt her? Her little arm looks so funny, all bent so funny."

"Barb, I'll go with you to the hospital. I'll come over and pick you up. We'll have a doctor look at your baby. You want to help her, don't you?"

"Yes, yes, I do."

"I'll be there in about ten minutes. Are you dressed?"

"How can I make her stop crying? She's still crying. I can't stand it!"

"Yes, you can, Barb. You just let her cry until I get there. Don't worry about her. I'll take care of her, and I'll take care of you, too. Why don't you sing a song until I get there? What was your favorite hymn when you were a little girl?"

"What?"

"What hymn did you love to sing when you were little?"

" 'Rock of Ages.' She's still crying."

"Okay, Barb, I want you to sing that song. Sing that 'Rock

of Ages' as loud as you can. Sing it three times. Don't worry about your baby; we'll take care of her later."

"I can't stand that damn crying." Her voice was becoming harsh, angry. I could still hear the baby's cries in the background, and I knew that they were adding to Barb's fear and frenzy.

"Pretend that Ali's singing. Set the buzzer on your stove. Can you reach it? Set the buzzer for fifteen minutes. Don't touch your baby until I get there. You can do it. I know you can."

"Okay, but she's still crying."

"That's okay, Barb, just let her cry. I'll ask Connie to call you while I'm on my way. Remember her telling you about what happened to her? She'll be good to talk to, won't she?"

"Yes. Okay. I guess so."

"When the phone rings, be sure to answer it. Okay, Barb? I want you to do three things—don't touch the baby, sing 'Rock of Ages,' and answer the phone when it rings. Okay?"

"Okay."

When I got to Barb's small upstairs apartment, she was desperately clutching the phone. On the other end of the line, Connie's voice was assuring her that everything would be all right. The baby was still crying; I picked her up and wrapped a blanket around her, being careful of her arm. Barb's eyes were frightened and sorrowful as she hung up the phone. She hovered over the baby, moaning her regret. I encouraged her to put on her coat, and we rushed down the stairs to my car.

The hospital was close by. Its emergency room was as usual. We filled out papers, which the nurses filed. A nurse and two police officers interviewed Barb. Then the hospital staff said that they wanted to keep the baby overnight for observation in case there were any head injuries as well as for treatment of the broken arm.

After it was all over, Barb and I went out to get something to eat, and for the first time that day, she was able to begin the process of finding out what had gone wrong. She clutched her coffee cup tightly and stared at her sandwich. I wanted to help her see that while the situation had been a bad one, she had, in the midst of what must have been great stress and pain, called for help. This was a hopeful sign.

"Barb, how are you? How are you feeling? What's been going on?" I asked.

"I'm numb; I'm just numb. This whole day, ever since my

boyfriend left, has been a fog. It hardly seems real. I don't know what I've done all day. Last night was so horrible. I keep going over and over it in my mind. It was awful! He always said he would leave me, and I was always scared he would. I was always so scared."

"Well, you don't have to be scared of that anymore."

Barb smiled stiffly and replied, "He left me plenty to remember him by, though. I'm so sore I can hardly sit here. I don't know what I'm going to do without him. Why did he leave? Why won't anyone marry me? Other people get married—ugly people, fat people. What's the matter with me? What am I going to do?"

"We can talk a lot about what you're going to do later. All of us in PA will be glad to share with you. I'm sure that there'll be some very good things happening for you. For now, though, let's talk a little more about you. What did you do after he left?"

"I waited for him to come back. I waited up all night for him to come back! But he didn't. I guess he meant it this time."

"Did you sleep at all or even lie down?"

"I lay on the couch for a while. It kind of hurt to lie down, but it kind of hurt not to, too."

"What about Ali through all of this? Where was she?"

"She was asleep in her bed, thank God."

"What else happened today, Barb? How was your afternoon?"

"The landlady was up for the rent again. I *hate* that lady—she hates me, and she hates my baby, my poor, sweet baby!"

Barb began to cry again. She wiped the tears away with the back of her hand. I passed her a paper napkin and waited while she gathered some stillness around her.

"What does the landlady do when she comes?" I asked.

"Every time she sees me, she makes some crack about my not paying the rent. I keep telling her I will. And I will, too. I don't expect to live there for free. I'll pay her her money. I don't have the money now, that's all. I got cut off the welfare rolls by mistake, the bastards."

Barb had been to the Parents Anonymous meeting the week before. She had been angry at the welfare system then, too. Being cut off had added one more layer of stress to her lonely life.

"That was last week, wasn't it? Have you been able to do

anything about it yet?"

"Yes, this morning I took Ali, and we went over to the welfare department to fill out the papers, those stupid papers. I *hate* having to beg, to prove what I need, even to prove who I am. I hate being pushed around like that, like I'm not even a person. Stand in this line, then that line! Fill out this, fill out that! I hate it! It took me forty-five minutes to get to that office on the buses. Then I had to wait for three hours. I had to stand in line for three hours! Then it took me forty minutes to get home."

"What did you do about lunch for you and Ali?"

"There wasn't anything I could do. I gave her a bottle, but I didn't know I was going to be there so long. I didn't have her food with me."

"What about you?"

"What about me?"

"Weren't you hungry?"

"No, I was okay."

"Did you have breakfast before you went?"

"No, my stomach still hurt."

"When did you last eat?"

"Just before he left last night, but then I threw up. He gave me a good punch in the stomach. I'd like to give him a good punch in the balls."

We both laughed. I reached over and touched Barb's hand and agreed, "I'll just bet you would. Did your baby cry while you were at the welfare department?"

"Yes, for the last hour and all the way home."

"That must have been hard on you."

"Huh? Yeah, I guess so."

"When you got home, what happened?"

"I gave her lunch. It must have been about three o'clock, and then I put her to bed."

"Did you try to take a nap, too?"

"No, I wouldn't have been able to sleep anyway."

"Aren't you awfully tired?"

"Huh? I don't know."

"Did Ali sleep?"

"Only for about ten minutes. Then the landlady came clumping up the stairs and yelled at me. I think she wakes up my baby on purpose; I hate her. It's not my fault. I'd pay her, but I just can't. I don't like her coming up and bugging me, though. It's my place. She rents it to me, and it's mine."

10

"What did you do after the landlady left?"

"Well, I cried for a while. I held my baby in my arms and cried for a long time. She's so soft, the sweet little thing. I love her so much!"

"Barb, at the PA meeting you came to, we talked a lot about knowing when to call for help. Did you think this might be the time you needed help?" I squeezed her hand again.

Barb shook her head. "No, I felt okay. I thought I was going to make it. I felt okay."

"Well, what happened next?"

"I took her to the grocery store. I didn't have any milk, and I had to have some milk for her. I had a dollar, and so I took it and went."

"Is the grocery store fairly close to you?"

"Yes, it's only about three blocks away."

"That must seem a lot farther when you're carrying a baby."

"It seems farther on the way back. On the way there I just snuggled Ali all the time, but on the way back, I had the milk, too. That's harder. I don't know how a little bit of a thing like Ali can weigh so much."

"You aren't very heavy yourself, Barb. You look as if you've been losing weight."

"Maybe I have. All this week, I haven't eaten. I've been upset. We've been fighting all week, and now he's gone. It's best, I guess, but it don't feel so great, I'll tell you."

"It still hurts, doesn't it? It isn't fun. It doesn't feel good at all." I guessed from Barb's reactions that something from her past was being reenacted. So I asked a standard PA question, "What does his leaving make you think of? Does it remind you of anything?"

"I don't know. What do you mean?"

"When you were little, who left you, Barb?"

"Everybody, everybody always left me. My father first. He beat us all so terrible, they put him in jail after he beat my brother to death, and they wouldn't let us see him. My momma says he didn't want to see us, but I think he did."

"He beat all of you? All your brothers and sisters?"

"Well, a little. My brother got it the worst, and after him, I always got it. I was the worst kid. My father said I reminded him of his mother, and she was no good and neither was I. He was right, I *am* no good, and I'm scared I'll kill Ali just like my father

11

killed Dave. I'm no good. I'm bad!"

"You can try to prove that to me later if you want, Barb. Right now, tell me, what would your father do after he beat you? While you were still crying, what would he do?"

"Sometimes he'd beat me until I stopped crying. I got so I hardly ever cried; everything would usually go all black instead. Other times he'd run from the house and say he'd never be back. Oh, I get it. *He* left, just like my boyfriend did! Is that what you meant?"

"Yes, that's what I meant. Did you think your father meant it about not coming back?"

"I was afraid he really *did* mean it. I wanted him to come back. I loved him so much."

"Even after he beat you?"

"I deserved it. It was my fault. I was bad! I'm still bad. I deserve to be killed for what I did to my own poor baby. I love her. I miss her so. I want to hold her and tell her how bad I feel. Do you think I can see her again tonight?"

"Yes, I think you can. Perhaps you'll want to stay in the hospital. Or maybe you'll want to go to Connie's for the night. I know she'd be glad to have you. Remember hearing how Anna had Connie over that time she needed help?"

"Yes, but she's made it. She's never hurt her baby again, just that once. She's all better. I never will be."

"Barb, Connie's been working on her problem for a year now. You've only begun. I promise you that in a year people will be saying that you're all better, too."

"But will I ever really be? Will I ever be all better?"

"That I don't know. But one thing I do know: you love your baby so much you're willing to work on this. Soon you won't be physically hurting your baby any more. You'll be doing better things with your feelings during hard times."

We picked up our purses and put on our coats. I paid the bill, and the two of us headed for my car. Before Barb could decide where to go for the night, I knew that she would need a few more moments to talk about her tormented day, so we sat together in the dark.

"Were you mad at your baby for crying?" I asked her.

"No, I wasn't. She was crying because she was ready for her dinner. It didn't bother me. But suddenly I was just out of control. I don't even remember what happened. I was just hitting and hitting, slapping and slapping. I was punching her, and I just couldn't stop! It was like my arms belonged to someone else, and they were the ones doing the beating. It seemed like it went on forever, and then I was just throwing her across the room. She was screaming and looking at me so scared. I should be killed. Who would hit a poor, innocent baby? She's my best friend, my only friend. I love her more than I love anything else in this whole world! Why would I hit my baby, my Ali?" Barb shut her eyes and hit her forehead with her clenched fist. Tears trickled down her face.

"People are kind of like pressure cookers, Barb," I said as I put my arm around her shoulders. "The more stresses and worries they put into themselves, the higher the pressure goes. If they don't take care of their feelings and do something about them, they'll eventually blow up, just like a pressure cooker will if you don't let the steam out. That's what happened to you today. Your feelings about being deserted again—this time by your boyfriend—and all the other feelings that piled up in you because of the welfare department and the long bus ride and the landlady and the empty refrigerator and the baby crying were just too much. You blew up. You didn't consciously *choose* to hit your baby; it just happened. It's a very bad way to handle feelings. There are other, better ways to handle them, and part of what we'll be doing in PA is to find out what other ways work for you."

"I don't even know what I feel," Barb confided. "Maybe I never did. I just know I feel like crying all the time. Why am I so sad?"

"Well, maybe that's one of the ways you handle those feelings which are all mixed up together. Or maybe you're sad because your boyfriend left you. You could tell me better than I could tell you."

"But I don't know."

"And you don't have the money for the rent. You put in quite a hard day trying to get it, though, didn't you?"

Barb nodded her head. She clutched herself with tense arms and slowly rocked back and forth, moaning softly, "I want to hold my baby."

"Barb, who held you when you were little?"

"No one. Sometimes my momma would hold me after she beat me. She was awfully sorry; she said she didn't know what got into her. I know though. It was me. I'm real bad, and I have to be beat. I should be beat now for what I did to my baby. You should beat me."

"Would that make your baby any better?"

"No."

"Would it make you any better?"

"I don't know. I know I deserve it, though."

"Nobody deserves it, Barb. Not you, not your baby. Nobody in this whole world deserves it. Because of what you're doing for your baby, because you're trying to get help in working through your feelings, your baby *won't* grow up like you did. Ali *won't* be beaten like you were when you were little. And when she grows up, she'll know better how to take care of her own feelings and her own babies because you're going to teach her something better. That should make you feel very proud, Barb. It makes me very proud of you. You really love that baby, don't you?"

"Yes, I do. I love her very much."

"And most of the time, you're good to her, aren't you?"

"Yes, I'm a very good mother except when I beat her."

I knew how hard Barb was trying to be a good mother—and I knew about some of the odds that were working against her. First, she herself had been abused as a child. Now that she had a child of her own, her life was so full of stress and anxiety that she reacted desperately to the pressures on her.

Although her baby, Ali, was five months old, she had been with Barb for only three months at the time of the abuse. One of Barb's problems was the fact that she was an unwed mother. This didn't bother her during her pregnancy, but while she was in the hospital she felt badly about not having a husband to visit her like other new mothers did. She also felt badly that she wasn't going to have someone to love her when she got home with her new baby. She became so depressed about her situation that she asked her sister to take care of Ali for a while; she wasn't sure that she would be able to function as a mother right away. So Ali lived with Barb's sister for two months, and this prevented the initial bonding that usually takes place between mother and daughter.

When Barb finally brought her baby home, she felt guilty for not having done it sooner. Many unspoken questions and doubts ran through her mind. She often wondered, "Does Ali love my sister more than she loves me? Is my baby mad at me for not bringing her home right after she was born?" In addition, Barb was still very uncertain about her ability to take care of a

14

new baby. She didn't know what to do or how to act. She didn't know how to diaper or feed Ali.

Barb tried to mother Ali out of a great emptiness. She felt incapable of being a good mother. She hadn't experienced good parenting when she was a child, so she had no idea of how to go about being a loving parent. She had no ongoing support from friends, either male or female. She was terribly lonely. And, finally, she had never known the security of positive self-esteem; she felt that she was a "bad" person and that she deserved whatever "punishment" she got.

On top of all of this, she was facing a whole realm of new feelings that scared her. Her love for her baby was strong, but so was her fear about her own behavior. After all, her father had killed his own son, her brother Dave. Would she kill her daughter?

That was what Barb's life was like when she first brought Ali home—a jumble of stresses and pressures, some real, some imagined, some old, some new. We've seen what it was like at the time when the abuse occurred—no money, no friends, no apparent way out. A year has passed since that episode. Today, there's no way that Barb would ever allow that many problems to pile up on her without stopping to deal with at least some of them. She can recognize the signs that lead up to abuse, and she can work with them constructively instead of destructively.

During the year following the abuse, Barb received ongoing support from Connie, who called her daily and supported her through her crises. Now Barb is the one who is calling other people. She is the one who is helping other parents to break their cycles of abuse. She tells them to call her any time, day or night. "I may be in the bedroom throwing pillows," she says, "but I'll be there!"

Barb is a great advocate of pillow-throwing. "It's cheap and fun," she smiles. "It feels good all along my shoulders, arms, and even across my back. A pillow makes a great sound when it hits the wall. I can just feel my tensions running down my arms and then flying through the air to crash into the wall. I feel so good that it's pillows I'm throwing these days! I'm a much better mother—maybe not perfect, but much better."

The story of Barb and her child Ali is a good example of what Parents Anonymous can share with people who need to know that abuse can be stopped. Barb was an abused child who grew up to become an abuser. She has managed to break that cycle of abuse. Parents Anonymous has given her some help, but she is also responsible for helping herself by bringing to PA her own determination to be a better parent than her own parents were. Barb never learned as a child or a teenager the necessary skills for coping with stress, but she's learning them now. And for Ali—and Ali's children—life will be different and better.

Barb is like most of the parents in this book. As children, they never had a chance to learn about adjusting to problems and dealing with them in a healthy way. How could they, when most of their lives consisted of physical and emotional battering or neglect? Adults who share their stories with PA today are likely to have much in common. They probably have very low self-images. They perceive themselves as bad. They have little or no respect for their own abilities. They don't problem solve efficiently because they simply don't see the alternatives open to them and and don't feel capable of shaping their own lives. They see themselves as basically powerless—as having no worth, no ability, and no choices. Many of them are desperate, and abuse is the act or the condition of desperation.

The type of abuse a person is involved in depends on a great many factors—the type of abuse the person experienced as a child, the amount of energy the person has, his or her physical health, the amount of support available to him or her, and the external and internal stresses of his or her own life, among other variables. It isn't that important, however, to understand how each type differs or who uses which type for what reasons. What is important is to understand that people who abuse are dysfunctional while they are abusing. They are dysfunctional as family members and dysfunctional as individuals. They must learn to function again; this is imperative. Only if they can learn to function regularly as human beings who are capable of caring for themselves and then for others will they be able to stop abusing. Abuse is as much a symptom as it is a problem.

Chapter 2
Defining Abuse

Injuries to children may be divided into two major categories: abuse (injuries resulting from actions *committed* by adults) and neglect (injuries resulting from actions *omitted* by adults). Abuse may be physical, emotional, verbal, sexual, or passive. Neglect may be physical or emotional.

Both abuse and neglect are harmful. Those of us who have examined the cycle of abuse and neglect do not consider any one form more harmful than another. Physical injuries hurt the body every bit as much as verbal and emotional injuries hurt the mind and spirit of a child. Neglect can scar a child as effectively as physical abuse. The abusive parents of today may have long since recovered from the physical injuries they suffered as children, but many are still emotionally crippled by the injuries they received to their feelings. These injuries do not heal like broken bones and cuts do.

Both parents and children easily recognize abusive episodes. They are explosive, dynamic, and intense. Abusive actions are the result of violent feelings. Most PA parents talk about being "out of control" when they abuse; they know when loss of control begins and when it ends.

Omitted actions are not as easily recognized, however. The feelings involved in neglect are neither as intense nor as powerful as those which are present during actual abuse. In addition, such occurrences usually lack clearly marked beginnings and endings.

This chapter deals with the four types of abuse, while Chapter 3 discusses neglect.

PHYSICAL ABUSE

Physical abuse occurs when an adult causes bodily injury to a child. Many PA parents feel that abuse also takes place whenever a parent hits or spanks a child while the parent is out of control. (The parent usually knows quite well whether or not he or she is in control.) The adult may administer the abuse by hand or with some object such as a belt, a wooden spoon, or an electrical cord. Some parents who use objects for disciplinary purposes do so because they cannot stand to touch their children. The feel of flesh on flesh is so repugnant to them that they use weapons instead.

Lisa, who called Parents Anonymous for help because she wanted her child returned to her (he had been placed in a foster home), is an example of a parent who physically abuses a child. Lisa is eighteen and shares some characteristics with other troubled parents. She herself is young—her baby was born when she was only seventeen—and she is alone much of the time. She was abused as a child, and she has a very poor self-image, but she loves her baby. She does not tolerate frustration well, and she has little control over her impulses. She acts upon her feelings before she has thought them through, and her actions seem to "happen" without her permission. Over the phone, Lisa's voice carried overtones of belligerence and stubbornness. While she wanted help, this was obviously a hard call for her to make. She had been covering up and trying to be tough ever since the court had removed her six-month-old child from her home two days ago.

"What can I say? I beat my kid.

"How often? Not very often; two or three times a week.

"How do I feel about it? I don't like it. Now what else do you want me to say?

"Just talk? What about?

"Anything at all? This is ridiculous! My baby is six months old. He had a broken arm when he was one week old, a broken leg when he was three months old, and now he has a fractured skull. You know all that. They told you, I know they did. When they took my baby, they said they were going to tell you. What else do you want to know?

"Just talk about anything? What anything?

"How do I feel? Well, I feel shitty. I felt shitty then and I feel shitty now. What the hell do you expect?

"You're right. We're not getting anywhere. I told you—no one can help me. I'm too far gone. It's too late for me and that baby. I won't ever get him back, and that's the best thing for him. He'll be much better off without me. I'm a shitty person.

"Will I miss him? Yes. Yes, I'll miss him.

"What will I miss about him? Oh boy, here I go. Old Toughie maybe isn't all that tough after all, but I'll try to tell you. I guess I want to say it. I've thought it, and now I want to say it. I'll miss the way he smells and the way he feels in my arms. I'll miss him because he was good company for me. I'll be bored without him. I always kept him with me. Wherever I went, I took him, too. Into every room I went, I took him. And you don't even need to ask that next question, then why did I beat him? Well, I'll tell you that, too. Why not. What difference does it make? Who cares anyway?

"Sometimes he'd start crying, and I couldn't get him to stop. He would cry and cry. I tried to be patient. Every time, I tried, but it didn't work. Well, sometimes it did. I didn't beat him every time he cried. But a lot of the time I did. It would seem as if his crying would get louder and louder until it filled the whole room. All I could hear was his crying. All there *was* was his crying. And then my skin would start to hurt, like his crying was little needles pricking and stabbing into my skin all over. The noise would pound into me. And then it would sound like it was getting higher and higher. And then I would start. I couldn't stop then; I knew I couldn't stop it then. No matter what, I couldn't stop it then. I was like a person in a trance. I knew I was doing it, but at the same time I didn't know it, if you know what I mean. I knew I was walking over to him, and I knew I was going to beat him, but I couldn't stop myself. His crying would go up and up and up, higher and higher. Then it would start to sound to me exactly like my mother's voice when she was screaming at me. It was *her* voice coming out of him; it was *her* screaming and screaming at me. I wouldn't hear him anymore, just her. I would feel her hitting me and all the while I was hitting him, but I didn't know it. I was hitting and hitting him, and she was hitting me, and he was screaming but it wasn't him, it was her screaming at me. And I had to shut her up. I had to shut her up!! SHUT HER UP!!!

"And then somehow I would start to calm down again. I would start to hear him again for a few seconds or so. Then it was her cry. Then I'd recognize him for a little longer. And finally it would be all him, and I'd be so exhausted and crying and back into myself again. He would be so sad and so scared and so hurt. Do you know, I remember just how he felt because I felt that way often; and I'd pick him up, and we'd rock and cry. I'd tell him how sorry I was and how much I loved him and how sorry I was, but he was still hurt. All my sorrow didn't make his bruises go away. You must think I'm crazy. Maybe I am."

Lisa isn't crazy, but like all adults who physically abuse children, she needs help in learning good parenting. She first needs guidance in identifying her own needs. She must learn how to fill them, how to recognize trouble signs, and how to find alternative ways of expressing her anger. Even with all the help in the world, though, can anything ever make up for what Lisa suffered through as a child? Those experiences are in large part responsible for the way she is today. Her wounds will never fully heal—but it's likely that she can learn to take the memories of her mother screaming at her and live through them constructively into the present.

It's hard to predict what will happen to her baby as Lisa works at separating the present from the past. How much chance is there that the two of them will ever be able to live happily together? How safe will her baby be with her—a month from now, a year from now? If the abuse continues, a foster home can be found—but for how long? And then what? It's possible that with proper care Lisa can learn to be a good mother to her baby, but it's also possible that she cannot.

Because physical abuse can and does result in severe injury or death, it is the form of abuse that has received the most attention from the general public and the media. When most people hear the term "battered child" or even the general term "abuse," they think of physical abuse. Many people believe that the physical form of abuse is the "real" one, but it is not the *only* real one: *all* forms of abuse are real. In fact, physical abuse is neither the most common nor is it always the most harmful type of abuse. Verbal, emotional, sexual, and passive abuse also leave scars that may last a lifetime.

VERBAL ABUSE

Verbal abuse is the use of words as weapons. The motive behind verbal abuse may not be injury, but the result surely is.

Most children have some feelings of inadequacy, but these natural feelings do not stultify them, lead them to hate themselves, or haunt all their actions for the rest of their lives. The message that a child is lousy, crummy, no good, and worthless, conveyed in repetitive doses daily and hourly, molds the child's self-image. The child grows up believing that he or she really *is* lousy, crummy, no good, and worthless. Verbally abused children have difficulty recognizing that they have worth, that they are valuable or good or loveable.

Verbal abuse occurs when an adult makes remarks to a child that are destructive to the child's self-image— remarks that are not aimed at the child's behavior as such, but rather at his or her sense of self-worth. No matter how casually harsh words are used, each does damage. Calling a child names day after day ensures that the child will grow up with a damaged self-image.

In general, angry or uptight parents find themselves using some of the very same words and/or phrases that their parents used on them when they were children. Words that are passed on in this way are usually very heavy, important words for both parent and child. An adult who was verbally abused as a child may only know one way to deal with his or her own child when the child does something the parent does not like.

Dee shared her experiences with this type of abuse with our PA group.

"I used to think it was better than hitting them, but now I'm not so sure. Every day of my life I was beaten, sometimes by my mother, sometimes by my father, sometimes by both. I've said to myself, *At least I'm not doing that to my kids.* But more and more lately I've been thinking about what really hurt me the most, what really hurts me the most now. You know, for all those beatings, I don't have one broken bone left, not one bruise, maybe a few scars [actually quite a few scars], but they don't show much. The problem I have now is that I know I'm no good. I know that because my folks told me I was no good so often that I believed them. You don't hear that all the time and not grow up believing it. That's my problem now. And that's exactly what I'm doing to my kids. I'm making them think they're no good.

"So I think maybe verbal abuse is worse than physical abuse. At least the physical stops; the verbal just goes on and on in my head. It never stops. When I get uptight at at my kids, or just uptight in general, when I lose control, the first thing I know I'm screaming at them. And I'm screaming every awful thing my parents ever said to me. Honest to God, the one thing I said I would never say is that they are whores, and every day I scream that at them. I open my mouth and out comes my mother. It's like I'm not even there. I don't even mean the stuff I say, I really don't even mean it. And sometimes afterwards I can't even remember what I was yelling about. I forget whatever it was, and I just yell and yell and yell. I'm so out of control then. Some days I can't even talk afterwards; I'm so hoarse I have to whisper. That's abuse, I know it is. It's abuse."

When her children upset her and Dee loses control, she calls them all sorts of names ("whore" being one of the less offensive terms she uses). The force of her rage and hate is so torrential during these episodes that she ends up using strong words in an effort to cleanse herself. She doesn't really mean the words she's saying, but using them relieves her tensions.

EMOTIONAL ABUSE

Emotional abuse is a side effect of every other form of abuse. It can be administered on its own, however, without the presence of any of the other types.

In emotional abuse the interaction between parent and child is thick with hidden feelings, veiled threats, whines for love, and references to past punishments and crimes. Emotional abuse creates a stifling and crippling atmosphere which is difficult to describe but easy to recognize. It severely damages the child's sense of self. It occurs when an adult uses weapons such as guilt or fear to influence a child's behavior. Parents who make their children feel so guilty that they can't leave home, for example, or who threaten illness, death, or desertion if their behavior doesn't change are emotional abusers. The flow of words and feelings is often insidious, but the total effect is devastating.

Although such a parent can and often does use harmful words against his or her child, it is the force of emotion *behind* the words which hurts the child the most. The child is left with feelings of inadequacy and helplessness.

Shirley's transformation of her own feelings into words, thoughts, and actions against her stepchild clearly demonstrate the devastating effects of emotional abuse.

"It's not fair, it's not fair, it's not fair! I washed that floor all morning; it took me three hours. I washed it on my knees. I always do it that way. And I waxed it the same way. Now he's gone and thrown his cracker on the floor. He's out to drive me crazy. I know he is. I don't even like him to eat between meals, but he kept saying he was hungry. I gave him a cracker and look what happened. He has no respect for me. He doesn't care what I go through. He only thinks of himself. He has got to learn some respect.

"His father says I don't love the boy. I take care of him, what more does he want? His clothes are clean and neat; at least I try to keep them that way. He's a very malicious child, though; he rips his clothes just to make it harder for me.

"Right now he's sitting on the couch in the other room. He'll sit there until bedtime and that might teach him something. He had no business being so clumsy with that cracker. I've told him over and over again not to spill things and not to make messes. His father says I'm too hard on him, that what he does is just an accident. How long am I supposed to put up with accidents? He'll stop having them when I teach him not to. He's four years old and that's old enough to learn. Actually, he's not quite four, but he will be. I'm not going to have him messing up the house for the next ten years. He's going to learn better.

"He's in there crying again. I told him not to cry, and he was pretty good for the first two hours, but now he's up to his old tricks. He's going to drive me crazy, which is exactly what he wants. He says he wants a toy. Well, if I let him have a toy, he'll just throw that around, too. I told him until he learns to be more careful, he's not getting any toys. I put them all away a week ago when he didn't pick them up.

"When his father gets home, he'll spoil him and let him off the couch. He's always working against me. Whatever I do or say, he does the opposite. He says I don't love the boy. I take care of him. He's been with us ever since one month after we were married. I thought we wouldn't have to have him for at least two years. He isn't even my child; he's his!

"It's been bad for us since day one, and it's gone downhill from there. I thought that when I got married I'd finally be happy. My parents were both alcoholics. They never had any time to take care of me. They weren't even home. I did everything in our house, not only for myself but also for my kid brother. They had him, and that was it. Even when he first came home from the hospital, I was the one who had to get up and feed him in the middle of the night. I kept him in my room. I had to dress him and feed him. I stayed home from school at least once a week to clean the house. It could have been a pigsty as far as they were concerned.

"My brother had terrible asthma, and sometimes I'd have to take him to the hospital. Then when I got home, I would get beaten for taking him. But he had to be taken care of, and they weren't going to do it. It was bad when they beat me, but then it was worse because they would beat him, too. That would make his asthma even worse, and then I'd have to hold him in my bed all night long. I won't have this kid in my bed, not ever.

"Yesterday morning he was eating his cereal with his fingers. It was disgusting. I won't waste money on milk for him to leave in the bowl any more, but still you wouldn't think he'd have to eat like an animal. So I said, 'Okay, you want to act like an animal, I'll treat you like an animal.' I gave him the cat dish

23

on the floor and now he has to eat his meals out of it on the floor. If he's going to act like an animal, he'll get treated like an animal.

"But his father will say I'm too hard on him. His father would give in to him all the time. He never does anything to correct him. He says it's because he feels so bad that the boy was beaten by his real mother. It's more than that, though. He's afraid to correct him, afraid to tell him to do anything. He won't even tell him to go to bed. I have to do it all. I always have to do it all.

"And it's such a bother; the boy is a bother. I make him stay in bed in the mornings until I have his father off to work. It's hard enough in the morning. Sometimes I have to wake his father up five times before he gets up. I get so upset, I throw up just trying to get him out of here on time. And the boy makes it so much worse, always calling on his father or me, anything to get an answer. I tell him, 'Just ignore the boy. He has to learn sometime. If you keep answering him, he'll just keep calling.' But he answers him anyway. He makes it so much harder for me. I have to teach that boy better. I have to be stricter with him."

Shirley's husband Roger made the first call for help. He seems scarcely more than a boy himself as far as his ability to give love is concerned, but he realizes that his family needs help.

Raised by alcoholic and severely abusive parents, Roger lacks both self-confidence and a sense of identity. He won't take part in disciplining his child; he doesn't want to get involved in anything unpleasant. He feels the same about fighting with his wife. His own childhood was so full of negative experiences— arguments, discipline, beatings, court sentences—that it's no wonder authority is a threat to him. By playing the role of a child, he forces Shirley to take care of the situation at home.

What can be done for couples like this one? First, they can be taught some specific child-management techniques. Roger can learn to accept some responsibility for his child, and Shirley can be given a better idea of what to reasonably expect from a three and a half year old. Marital counseling might help them to work better together. Shirley and Roger are very difficult to work with, however. They seem self-pitying and bitter much of the time. They are neither motivated to change, nor are they very loving to their child. What they are doing is almost impossible to tolerate and almost as hard to change. But if they receive the care and attention they need during their crisis moments, then perhaps—just perhaps—they might move from where they are into a new and better place. What love they now have for themselves and their child is a pale and watered-down reflection of their own feelings of weakness, insecurity, and inadequacy. With care, they just might be able to move to a place where they can love each other and their child with strength and warmth.

Although the present doesn't look too good for their child, chances are that he will still be better off than either of his parents. Shirley and Roger are not alcoholics, and so they are providing a somewhat simpler situation than the one they grew up with. Their son is never physically abused, as both of them were as children. But the emotional abuse he is sustaining at this time may turn him into another emotional cripple. Shirley, Roger, and their son all need care and support.

PASSIVE ABUSE

The passive abuser never actually lays a hand on the child, but he or she is just as involved in the abuse as if he or she had personally inflicted it. The passive abuser paves the way for abuse; he or she sets it up and allows it to occur. There is no such thing as a family in which one parent abuses and the other parent is completely uninvolved or ignorant of it. In an abusive family, everyone is involved, and everyone is responsible to some extent.

Instead of acting out his or her own feelings, the passive abuser manipulates someone else into acting them out. Someone else vents the frustration, the anger, the resentment; someone else hits the child. The feelings of passive abusers may be submerged, but they are not weak; they are simply released through other people. Passive abusers find it impossible to express their own feelings. They are often so unaware of their own feelings that they insist they don't have them at all. The only relief they get is when they can manipulate someone else into expressing their feelings for them.

Carolyn and Jeff illustrate the type of relationship which often exists between active and passive abusers. It wasn't until after Carolyn had stopped physically abusing their five children that Jeff would even discuss the fact that he had been a passive abuser. He didn't believe in talking about his problem. He believed that if you had a problem you either did something about it or you didn't. If you did something about it, there was no need to discuss it. If you didn't do anything about it, there was no sense in discussing it.

When he and Carolyn were engaged and even when they were first married, they talked a lot but they never really communicated their feelings. With five children, the opportunities for talking got lost. Jeff is having a hard time right now because he has forgotten what little he once knew about talking about his feelings. He is mystified by the changes that have occurred in Carolyn and in his relationship with her since she began coming to Parents Anonymous meetings.

"When she told me I was a passive abuser, I knew I didn't understand her at all any more. I don't know what's happened to her. I don't know what I'm supposed to do or how I'm supposed to react. I don't know what's going on inside her, and brother, it ain't because she don't tell me often enough. But *what* is she talking about? I just don't understand. She isn't the same person she was a year ago. And I don't know what to do.

"I come home from work, and sometimes she's only gotten home herself. I ask her, 'Where's dinner?' She says, 'I just got home.' I know that; I see that; but I want to know where's dinner.

"So I ask her, 'Are you going to make dinner?' And she says, 'Oh, no, you're not laying a guilt trip on me. I'm not going to have you make me feel guilty.' Who the hell was talking about guilt? I was talking about dinner.

"And a little later, I ask her where she was all day. She says, 'I don't have to answer to you anymore.' I don't exactly remember asking who she was answering to. I want to know where she was. So I get pissed, and I sit there not saying much. She gets up and says, 'I'm going out, I'm not going to sit here while you glare at me. The kids are all in bed now and I'm going out.' The hell she is! I get a little angry. In fact, I get a lot angry at her, and I chuck her up against the garage wall. I don't even know I'm doing it until she's there. She goes—get this—she goes, 'Well, that was honest anyway.' This dumb broad gets tossed up against the wall, and then she tells me I'm honest. I don't get it.

"And it's all kinds of things. She never used to let me touch the kids. And now she says, 'If the kids are bad around you, you spank them. Don't always be calling me to do it.' She says I don't know how to express my feelings for myself. She says

26

I make *her* express them for me. She says I act uptight, and then I nag her until finally she explodes and it's usually at the kids.

"Then after *she's* blown up at the kids, I feel better, she says. That really blew my mind. I started to get mad just listening to her, and that kind of scared me. I got scared of what I felt like doing to her.

"And she says she wants to talk about anger. What makes me angry now? What used to make me angry? I say, 'Shut up!' I say it because I don't know what makes me angry now and I don't want to find out.

"But she keeps coming back to anger, at least it seems that way to me. How was it when I was little? I can remember getting angry a couple of times. I went into a rage, a real rage. I wrecked everything I could get my hands on, and I could have killed anybody. I'll tell you. I could kill; I know I could.

"I don't remember getting angry for a very long time now. Oh, maybe a little bit upset every now and then, a little uptight, but usually I just ignore it, and it goes away. Carolyn says it doesn't go away; she says she takes it for me. She says I go around looking to give my mad away; that it's like I put it in a brown paper bag and hand it to her. She says her mistake has been in taking it and she's not doing it no more. I don't know what she's talking about.

"She keeps talking about the day I supposedly nagged her so much that she abused Peter. She told me, 'I did it for you, you know. You wrapped up all your anger and you passed it straight over to me and I, like a dutiful wife, took it all, and I BLEW UP and I hurt Peter!'

"That's what she said and I think I understand a little of what she means; but I don't know what to do. I don't know what there is to do."

His experiences as a young child taught Jeff that people expressed their feelings only when they were drunk. He learned that feelings in his family had more to do with alcohol than with people, and so he never learned to respect feelings. He minimized and distrusted the feelings of the people around him and minimized and distrusted his own feelings in turn. He learned early to cover up his reactions. He wanted his mother to stop talking to him about how she felt, and so he became quiet and unresponsive.

When Jeff and Carolyn got married, they had an unwritten contract to downplay the emotional side of their relationship. As the children were born (and the five of them came along rather quickly), Carolyn became more and more withdrawn as she tried harder to keep her feelings hidden. Jeff, on the other hand, became increasingly demanding. He discovered how best to manipulate Carolyn, which remarks would elicit which reactions from her. Finally, when one of their children was seriously hurt, they were forced to seek help.

Looking at and talking about their relationship with each other and with their children soon became vitally important to Carolyn. She insisted that they talk about their feelings. Jeff was terrified. He was understandably concerned about removing his feelings from their protective coverings.

As Jeff learned to recognize and express his feelings, anger was the first one to overflow. He expressed it inappropriately and destructively by hitting his wife. They were both shocked. The next time he hit Carolyn, she made it clear that he had not yet found the permissible way to express his anger. Once both manipulation and actual abuse of his wife were forbidden to him, Jeff turned on the children. That was also forbidden, both by the school, who reported him for child abuse, and by Carolyn, who said flatly that she would not allow him to hurt the children. Jeff is presently struggling to find constructive ways of expressing his newly acknowledged feelings. He still has a long way to go, but the journey has at least begun.

SEXUAL ABUSE

Sexual contact between an adult and a child constitutes sexual abuse. Beyond that generality and commonality are many variables. Sexual abuse may or may not involve penetration, intercourse, ejaculation, and/or orgasm. (Actual penetration of young children is rare, primarily because the sizes of the child's vagina and anus and the adult penis are incompatible.) Sexual abuse is usually inflicted on a female child by a male adult, but it may also occur between male and male, female and male, or female and female. It may take place between one male and one female, or many different males and one female, such as in a family where the male members have gotten the message that sexual abuse is okay. It may also occur between one male and more than one female, such as a father and several daughters.

Sexual abuse is always the last form of abuse to be admitted and discussed. More condemnation is attached to it than to any other form, yet less is known about it. It is very difficult to understand and help sexual abusers; few guidelines exist. For the most part, too little knowledge exists to offer even the victim helpful security in a nonjudgmental way. The enormous amount of feelings and emotions which surround sex in general—and sex with children in particular—not to mention sex between members of the same family and forcible rape all contribute to the problem of dealing effectively with the perpetrators and victims of sexual abuse.

Sexual abusers generally have poor sexual relationships with their mates, poor relationships with people in general, and poor marriages. They also have very poor perceptions of how what they are doing affects their children. Some tenderness may or may not accompany the abuse, but the child will suffer a trauma regardless. Sexual contact between a sexually mature adult and an immature child is by its very nature traumatic to some degree, and its effects may range from mild to severe.

Increasing quantities of evidence indicate that sexual abuse is far more common than has been suspected in the past. Many parents who once only talked about the physical abuse they suffered as children are now also talking about the sexual abuse; however, most people are still unable to discuss it freely and openly. Gerard is an exception; he has had to learn to talk about it.

"Well, the big thing was that communication between my wife and myself was really gone. I mean it just wasn't there. That sounds simple, really simple, but that's where it was at. We never talked. I knew I was needing something, but I didn't know what it was. I couldn't tell that, I just knew I was hurting.

"One night I went into my daughter's room to rub her back. She was thirteen. She was wearing a brace at the time, and she had taken it off, and I went in to massage her. That's okay, I'm her dad. Well, when I touched her, I found out through my hand that that was what I had been wanting. It was the touch, the feel of the closeness of her. The only time I ever touched my wife was when we were having sex, and we didn't do that very often. There's more to touching than sex. I could go to a prostitute if sex was what I wanted, but I'm not that kind of a guy. That wasn't what I wanted. Screwing isn't the answer to being close. It's part of it; it's very special; but it isn't the answer. It was the closeness I wanted—the closeness I was feeling with my daughter. My daughter and I have always been very close.

"Well, I started to rub her, and then I kind of lost control, and I was rubbing her all over, and then I was having oral sex with her. Once I found out what I was doing, I couldn't stop. I went to a priest to talk about it and try to figure out a way to stop. I knew it was wrong. He told me to say ten 'Hail Mary's,' ten 'Our Father's,' and to stay out of her room. Well, that didn't do it for me, if you know what I mean. It was with her that I felt the only love and closeness that I ever felt in my life. That was hard to want to give up. I guess I was kind of getting back at my wife, too, at least after it started. I knew there was some of that there, too.

"I started laying all kinds of trips on my daughter. I told her it was our secret, that if she told, they'd call the police and I'd have to go to jail, that we'd have to sell the house and get a divorce and our family would be broken up and it would be her fault. I also told her I loved her and I'd take care of her. I said I'd be the man around the house, and I'd be the one in charge, and I'd have all the answers for her. It felt good to her, too, so she wasn't going to tell anyone. What finally happened was that she wrote about it in her diary, and someone found it and read it and turned it in to the school. That happened about a year after we got started.

"It was really earth-shattering for me then, I'll tell you. I lost my job, we had to sell our house, and I did get a divorce. It was really painful. I mean, we hadn't had much of a marriage, but I did love my wife.

"Well, things are better for me all around now. That would never happen to me again. I know how to talk about my feelings; I know how to communicate with people. Touching is important, but I know how to touch now. And I'm a better parent now. I've always been a good parent, I think, but now I'm a better one. I give my kids a chance to talk about their feelings, too."

Children who are sexually abused, especially in ongoing relationships with adults in their own family, have no "safe spaces" in their lives. Even their bedrooms and their sleep are violated, and there is no protection or hiding place for them. Some women who were sexually abused as children have disturbed sleeping patterns as adults. They may routinely wake many times during the night, generally with a start, and then fall back to sleep. They may be more comfortable sleeping during the day or napping than sleeping through the night. They may choose late bedtimes and learn to live with little sleep.

   Children who are sexually abused are unable to trust anyone fully. Because they were unable to trust as children, they experience difficulty trusting others as adults. In PA, they begin the process of learning to trust.

Chapter 3
Defining Neglect

Both legally and morally, neglect is considered to be a form of abuse. Clinically it can be differentiated, but because the result of neglect is so obviously negative, it rightfully has been classified as abuse.

PHYSICAL NEGLECT

Physical neglect, as its name implies, is exactly that—the neglect of the physical needs of the child. Failure to provide medical attention, proper meals, adequate and appropriate clothing, and routine body care constitutes physical neglect. Children need to be cared for and they have a right to this care.

As with all types of abuse, physical neglect is a sign that something is wrong in the parent's life. Physical neglect demonstrates that for some reason, such as a recent divorce, a death, or more complicated personality problems, the parent is not taking adequate care of the child.

Parents who neglect their children often neglect their homes as well. Lydia was such a person. Her house was filthy. The odor from the dog, cat, and hamster and their waste was overpowering. The stale food odor from the sinkful of dirty dishes and the stale body odor from the loads of dirty clothes piled in the laundry room, kitchen, and bedrooms, made it hard to think of anything but not throwing up in her house.

Some professionals who work in the area of child abuse believe that neglecters are harder to treat than abusers. However, the people who have neglected their children disagree with this bold viewpoint. They say that neglecters have the same needs and the same abilities as any other parent in need of special help. Perhaps it's closer to the truth to say that neglecters are not "harder" to treat; rather, they require different treatment. Unlike abusive parents, the energy level of neglecting parents is often so low that for them even to get to appointments with their therapists is practically impossible and, therefore, treatment falters at that early point. The therapist may need to make many home visits in the beginning.

Frequently, adults who neglect their children are so full of and enervated by their own problems that they have no energy to spare. Typically, the neglecter has very little drive or initiative and lacks both motivation and the desire to follow through. The adult caught up in a pattern of physical neglect may alternate long periods of sleep with times when he or she sleeps sporadically or not at all. This type of person rarely goes out of the house and has few, if any, close friends. Just *living* seems to be the extent of the coping ability of the adult who physically neglects.

Betsy, whose energy level was very low, was able to get some help. In the midst of changing, Betsy reflected on how she had physically neglected her children.

"It wasn't that I wouldn't take care of them. It was that I *couldn't* take care of them. I love those little guys. I always did. It didn't have anything to do with love; I just couldn't handle them. Loving them didn't get diapers changed or meals made. I just couldn't handle that stuff. I would forget them—the kids, I mean. I slept and slept, and I didn't even think of them. I didn't hear them when they cried. My old man would come home, and they'd be crying, and I wouldn't even have heard them. Not even have heard them! I wasn't ignoring them on purpose or anything like that; I just couldn't get it together enough to take care of them. I didn't change their diapers all day, but it didn't seem that way. They had big red sores all over their bottoms, but it seemed like I changed their pants a lot. I felt terrible about it when I looked at them, but that didn't do any good. I guess I gave them custodial care and not very good custodial care at that. I didn't have the strength or energy to do anything else. I couldn't give what I didn't have.

"My dear, darling departed—my ex-husband—was in and out, mostly out. I never knew when he would come home and what shape he would be in when he did come home. We fought something terrible. There were some good times, but mostly it was bad. We fought more and more. He used to beat me. Right in front of the kids, he used to beat me. That's not something kids should be seeing; that's wrong. But I didn't know how to stop it.

"One time I decided to kill myself. I thought it would be better if I just did away with myself and saved us all some grief. I wasn't doing anyone much good anyway the way things were. So I went into the bathroom and took most of a bottle of Excedrin. But after I took them, you know what I thought? You know what flashed into my head? *If I do this, who is going to make Dudley's cereal in the morning?* Isn't that ridiculous? It never occurred to me until right then. *Who would take care of Dudley the next morning?* I threw the rest of the bottle of Excedrin as hard as I could up against the wall. It smashed all to pieces, and there was Excedrin all over the floor, the shelves, and everything. I was so pissed at those pills, at that bottle, that I just let them stay there. We had Excedrin on the floor for weeks after that; we just stepped over them, and sometimes we stepped on them. I felt so bad the next day I never did make Dud's cereal. I just gave him a bottle.

"It was like that a lot. My kids haven't always had three square meals a day. Sometimes we went for a long time without a regular meal. You'd never believe it to look at me, I know. But it's true. And I don't like it. But I couldn't get it together to cook a meal or to clean house. I'd rather sleep, and there really didn't seem to be anything else worth doing.

"Do you have any idea of what it's like to have no energy? I mean, absolutely zip, *no* energy? The kind where to move from the couch to the bathroom is all you can manage for a whole morning? Well, it's not fun. Even to breathe seems like a job, and thinking is impossible. It's like being in a thick soupy pool inside and out, no way to do anything, nothing to see, nothing to think, heavy nothing, can't even get hold of that.

"I knew I wasn't taking good care of the kids. I couldn't get them dressed; they smelled. Sometimes we didn't go out for days.

"I went for help. But I couldn't even be honest with my therapist, or at least I wasn't. I told her some of my shit, but not enough. I mean, how stupid is that? You go for help and then you don't even tell her all the shit. I didn't tell her how it was with my kids. I didn't want to lose them. I was afraid she might take them away from me. I wanted to be all better. I wanted to have the house clean and the kids taken care of. I wanted that to happen. But I didn't want to talk about all my shit. I couldn't handle it.

"God, especially I didn't want to talk about my childhood. I said I didn't remember it. And that's partly true. I don't remember a lot about it; there are great chunks of it gone. Gone, totally gone. But I do remember some things and I don't like those things very well. The happiest year of my childhood was the year I spent at a home for abused kids. I was coming from some pretty raunchy stuff and to have some order and stability put into my life was great.

"I didn't much want to talk about my marriage, either. The best thing that guy ever did for us was to leave us, I know that. But you know what? When he did leave us, I got strung out. I mean up and down the walls. That was when I had my little spin-out! I couldn't keep it together at all then. My sister took the kids for a few days. It was going to be longer, but she had their hair cut. I was furious! *Nobody* cuts *my* kids' hair but *me*. *I am their mother. I* will get their hair cut when *I* think it should be cut. They had beautiful hair. But she thought it was too long, and I guess it was dirty then. But I was furious, and I told her to get those kids back right now. She did, too. I guess that 'mad' was the energy I needed to get unspun from my spin-out.

"Like I said, it was the best thing he ever did, to leave us. But you know what? It tore me up inside. I knew he wasn't any good; but if that man who wasn't any good would leave *me*, what did that mean about *me*? That I was worse than no good? I thought that might be true. So I went to sleep. I didn't like it—the way I was living—but I didn't like much anyway so what was the difference? I couldn't handle getting left and I didn't know why.

"I know a little better now. I've thought a lot about it, and remembered some shit. When I was a kid, my mother would say I was no good, which I believed; that I wasn't even her kid, which I was; that she didn't love me and that she was going to get rid of me. She would take me to a public housing development near us and leave me. Do you have any idea of what it feels like to be left? I thought it was all my fault because I was so bad. Who would want me if she didn't? I don't like to think about it.

"But the energy I spent *not* thinking about it used up my energy from other places, like taking care of the kids. Isn't that crummy? All my life I wanted to be a mother, but when the time came, I couldn't do it. I just couldn't do it."

It was the *not* dealing with things that kept Betsy immobile. The energy required to keep from thinking of her childhood and her marriage and her parenting and her personhood kept her asleep. But she slowly realized that sleeping didn't solve her difficulties, so she began to attack her problems by coming to PA. As the weeks passed, she became more active and began to interact more with her children. Because of interaction—a new thing in her relationship with her children—she began to neglect less and abuse more. But Betsy continued to deal with her problem areas, and she learned to stop abusing her children. She now does no physical abusing and only infrequently abuses verbally and emotionally. Her neglect has almost totally ceased. Betsy is continuing to learn how to interact positively, both with her children and with other people.

36

EMOTIONAL NEGLECT

Emotional neglect is the neglect of the emotional needs of the child. Passive indifference surrounds a child who is being emotionally neglected; even the irritation and resentment his or her parents may be feeling are often submerged and kept hidden. Parent and child are involved in a quiet nonrelationship. The parent is unwilling or unable to be emotionally present to and involved with his or her child.

Emotional neglect differs from emotional abuse in that nothing harmful is actually said or done to the child. In fact, not enough is done, period. The adult doesn't seem to dislike or hate the child in any way; the child awakens few feelings, either negative or positive, in the parent. Often emotional neglecters are not even aware of the fact that they are not doing a very good job of parenting.

Children who have been emotionally neglected seem to grow up with an unclear or vague idea of who they are. Many don't perceive themselves as being good or bad; they simply don't perceive themselves as being anything at all. Most adults who were emotionally neglected as children have a great deal of trouble learning to trust themselves or to respect their own feelings. It is hard for them to develop a belief in their own integrity and worth. They will say, "I just don't feel anything. Not anything, just blank empty inside." As children, they perceived that they had no effect on their parents; as adults, they view themselves as nonentities.

Neglect in its most extreme form results in the "failure-to-thrive" infant—a baby who both physically and emotionally does not develop normally. Babies need contact with their parents. They need caring, emotional contact, not just the minimal contact of feeding and changing. Babies without adequate stimulation, handling, and love do not thrive. While emotional neglect of any form leads to underdevelopment of some aspect of the child, infants graphically show the actual failure-to-thrive syndrome.

Failure-to-thrive infants may begin as undemanding babies; even if they don't, they're forced to become that way. When their needs are never met, they stop making them known. They cry seldom or for only brief periods of time because they've learned that nothing happens when they do cry. Parents brag about what "very good" babies these infants are because they never cause any "trouble." A failure-to-thrive infant can grow and change from a listless, thin baby into a fat, lively one in a few weeks in a hospital setting where the attendants respond to his or her needs.

Jenny, a beautiful young woman who emotionally neglected her infant daughter, Patti, tells about her experience:

"Well, first off, it seemed it was her; she was so small. She just didn't gain weight. She'd gain maybe an ounce or so every time I took her to the doctor, but that's all. Every time, just a bit, and then after a while, nothing. Her brother, he gained too fast. But her, nothing. She seemed to eat okay, when I fed her, but she never cried. She didn't laugh, just lay there. It was okay with me because I had plenty going on inside me, but still she didn't seem right. I just had a funny feeling about her, nothing specific, but something...

"I wasn't home much with her or with her brother. Not that I left them: I didn't. I took them with me when I went out. My mom and my two sisters live real close to me, and I would spend a lot of time with them. We live in a public housing project and it's handy for us all. I'd help do their work. I'd do a lot for them. I'd clean for my mom, and I'd cook for her, and I'd always have my sisters' kids, sometimes all of them. I did everything for them—shopping, bathing—everything. I must've been nuts! I didn't even have a car, and I'd walk to the store with my two kids and usually some of theirs, just to buy stuff for them.

"All the while, my baby, my own daughter, was just lying there getting worse and worse. But I didn't notice too much. She was so quiet and good; she just lay there, looking around with those beautiful eyes of hers. She has the biggest eyes I ever saw. She didn't laugh or cry; she was just so solemn all the time. It was kind of weird how she would just lie there and look with those big soft eyes, looking and looking.

"I knew there was something wrong with her, but I didn't know what. I kept asking my mom and my sisters. They just said, 'No, she's just good, that's all.' But I knew it was more than that. I didn't think about it, though, if I could help it, and I usually could. I just went somewhere. I didn't like being home alone with the kids. I would do anything to avoid that.

"My family didn't understand at all. They never thought about why I might be there with them so much instead of at home. It was okay though, I probably couldn't have told them. They're always telling me how dumb I am. I try to tell them anything, and they start in with the dumb stuff again. Why do they always pick on me? There are lots of us in the family, why always me?

"I've asked myself 'why' a lot lately. I wonder why I had to do so much for them and why I didn't bother with my own kids. I think I didn't bother with them maybe because they were part of me and I knew I wasn't important, so they weren't important either. For sure they weren't as important to me as my mother or sisters. I wanted my mom to like me, so I'd work for hours for them to prove to her that she should like me. Isn't that silly? Here I'm a mother myself, doing all this stuff to get my mother to like me!

"And really I didn't like being home alone with the kids either. It was too lonely and too quiet. With their father gone, it's even lonelier and quieter. At least he's supposed to be gone. This morning he was trying to get in my window at 6:00. I let him in. I want him to see his kids sometimes. They're his kids, too. And also what am I going to do? I don't want to fight. How do I know how he is? What if he's high or stoned or something? I've had enough black eyes and bleeding teeth to last me a lifetime.

"My family has been giving me a rough time about letting him in, but they always give me a rough time anyway. Like the day I found out my daughter's problem was *me*, they were no help. I walked out in front of a truck that night, and the next thing I knew it was three weeks later. I'd been drinking, of course, what else did I do? Then in the hospital I thought about all the things I had done to my kids, but more than that, I thought about all the things I *hadn't* done for my kids. They just weren't very important to me. I had better things to do than think about them, like go to jail for fighting with police in bars, right? So I end up in the hospital with my daughter nearly dying in front of my eyes. Well, that's not going to happen again. I'm going to do a lot of things differently now. They're going to be important to me. I'm going to think about them for a change."

Because she was emotionally neglected by Jenny, Patti became a failure-to-thrive infant. Jenny spent so much time trying to meet her own needs that she had no energy left for her child. All of her efforts were in vain, however, since she received no support from anyone else—not her husband, her mother and sisters, or her friends. This was a very difficult situation that proved impossible for Jenny to handle on her own.

Patti had always been undemanding; Jenny talked often

of how "quiet" and "solemn" and "good" Patti was. This apparently "good" behavior only added to the problem. A passive and quiet baby who lies still for long periods of time gets little attention, and as even less attention is shown, the baby becomes quieter still. Patti got little attention from her mother, and Jenny got few positive feelings from her interactions with Patti because the baby was unresponsive and as a result probably not very interesting to Jenny. No real attachment or bonding between mother and child occurred.

Besides, Jenny had enough problems to deal with—her drinking, her family, and her marriage. She could identify her problems, but she didn't know what she needed to begin to solve them. Since Jenny couldn't meet her own needs, she certainly couldn't trust her ability to meet other people's needs. Her baby daughter and her small son weren't much help; they had both been conditioned to be undemanding. When Jenny became convinced that she was a failure as a mother, this made trusting her abilities with the children even harder. Jenny felt most inadequate when she was at home alone with the children, so she did her best to avoid the situation by leaving the house as often as possible and taking them with her. She lavished the attention her children should have received on her mother and sisters.

Finally, Jenny began to realize the price of avoiding her responsibilities as a mother. Once she saw that Patti was paying that price, she decided to learn how to be more successful at mothering her own children. It's a difficult road, but she's on her way.

Chapter 4
The Cycle of Abuse

Most people repeat some of their childhood experiences in their adult lives. Each of us is programmed from an early age to react in certain ways to certain types of situations. This programming seems to be strong and enduring. The experiences that people have already lived through are the realities they know best. They recreate these experiences because they literally know no other way to respond. The past shapes the present, and the familiar can be comforting. Adults do not always play the same roles they played as children, but they do tend to set up situations in which the same roles can be played out.

Most parents who abuse their children have had difficult or traumatic childhoods. Thus, their psychological health is often severely impaired. Their concepts of themselves, their worlds, and their families often evidence their inadequate mental well-being as adults. Their past traumatic experiences have shaped and crippled their present emotional response patterns. They are inadequately prepared to respond in healthy ways to life situations and often manipulate their environments to simulate their own childhood tragedies. After all, their only first-hand knowledge of how to respond to their children or to their spouses, to stress or to new problems, is what they learned as children from abusive parents who also had inadequate response patterns.

Beth lives in fear that she will abuse her child again and have to rehospitalize him. As a child, she suffered through verbal, physical, and emotional abuse. Today, she bears the scars of her childhood and continues the cycle which was probably set up by some distant ancestor. Until quite recently, she continued to recreate her own past as she interrelated with her five-year-old son.

As an adult, Beth is certain that she does nothing right. She perceives her ideas as immature, her abilities as inadequate, and herself as unworthy. If she doesn't understand a situation or a statement, Beth is reluctant to say so, for she considers any lack in herself as her own fault. She is unwilling to ask for clarification because she is sure that her questions will annoy and anger the people around her. She feels lost in the vastness of her "dumbness" and powerless to live effectively within her "stupidity." Beth believes that she is a failure as a thinking human being.

Beth doesn't recall becoming conscious of how "dumb" she is. Stupidity has been a part of her self-image for as long as she can remember. But Beth does recall certain incidents which stand out for her as painful proof of her "dumbness." One in particular is etched in sorrow.

"I was making Christmas cookies with my mother. We didn't do a lot of things together, but we did do some, and making Christmas cookies was one of them. I got to do the cutting, and then she put the cookies on the cookie sheet. Since I was almost five at the time, I was allowed to help her stir and measure for the first time. I can remember how the kitchen smelled, kind of wet and warm and sweet. I felt really good. It was snowing outside, and Gramma was coming for dinner to have our new cookies for dessert.

"My mother told me to go and measure out a pint of something. I don't even remember what it was, but I do remember the feeling in the pit of my stomach. I got this horrible feeling. I had no idea what a pint was. I kind of stood there for a minute—it was a very long minute. I knew I was going to ruin everything, that this was the end of our good time. Finally, I told her I didn't know which one the pint was. I'll never forget having to say that. She was standing there right in front of me with the rolling pin in one hand, and she picked up the cookie sheet in her other hand. I just stood there. She hit me first with one and then with the other and then with both of them at the same time. She yelled and screamed at me—how stupid I was—how no good I was—how dumb I was—how bad and useless I was—how ugly and stupid I was. I just stood there. I was right. I had ruined it.

"I can still see the corner where I was standing. And I can see how it changed when I was kind of huddling there. I can see the colors of the wallpaper, the design on the floor. I can even see the way the design changed as my tears got in the way. I don't know how I can remember so much about it, but I do. I hate red to this day—that's what color the wallpaper was in that corner.

"I still get that same sick feeling every time I don't know something, as if she's still standing over me with a rolling pin and a cookie sheet and I'm going to get it."

Beth has those same fears and feelings to overcome today when she doesn't know the answer she "should" know or when she knows there is a question to ask but is unable to formulate it. She has been well conditioned to believe that she's "dumb" and to get those feelings of inadequacy in the pit of her stomach whenever she doesn't know something. Every day, she must do energetic battle against those old feelings.

Recently Beth viewed her past Christmas experience with a new and clearer insight gleaned from her daily struggles to become a good parent.

"It didn't mean I was stupid just because I didn't know what a pint was, did it? I don't expect my five year old to know everything. I don't expect anybody to know everything, except me. My mother might have been wrong to expect that from me. Maybe I didn't know that just *yet,* but it didn't necessarily mean that I was stupid."

For Beth to express that realization was a gigantic step for her to take. She's not quite sure she believes it all the time, or even that she believes it some of the time, but it's enough for now that she's willing to admit that her mother *might* have been wrong and that she herself is not necessarily stupid. Beth's lifelong belief in her own worthlessness is weakening moment by moment as she insists on her right to be and on her existence as a person who can make her own choices and decisions.

When Jimmy called PA the first time, he, too, had feelings of worthlessness.

"I'm a lousy father, a really shitty dad. I can't father my children at all. They'd be better off without me. If I never came home again, it'd be great for the whole family. I love my kids, but I think I have a cruel streak somewhere in me or something like that. I can't explain it. I never was any good with words, especially trying to talk about something like this.

"The minute I get home, I start in on the kids, especially the oldest one. It seems to me he can't do anything right. Whatever he's doing, I start yelling at him for not doing something else or for not working harder or better. I just yell and yell at him, and then sometimes I start to hit him. I get so out of control I'd like to sock him right in the mouth. If he ever tries to do anything nice for me, I just can't accept it. I pick and pick until if I were him, I'd wish I'd never even heard of my dad.

"I mistreat him the worst, but I mistreat them all. I even mistreat the dog sometimes, just because, I don't even know why. I think I really do have a cruel streak." Jimmy's feelings of worthlessness differ from Beth's. He doesn't necessarily believe that he *himself* is bad, but that his *feelings* are bad. This is what his parents taught him, and he has carried it through into his own adulthood.

When Jimmy was a child, he was allowed to cry only if he went to a particular corner of the basement where he couldn't be seen or heard. His parents wanted him to be "tough," to be a "man," and firmly believed that men don't make their feelings obvious. They didn't want to be bothered with a child's emotions. Jimmy heard again and again when he was growing up that his feelings were "wrong," so he thinks that his feelings today are also "wrong." The fact that he was able to talk about his feelings over the phone to a PA member was a step in the right direction. He loved his children, or he wouldn't have called. He is beginning to be able to show his feelings more and expects others to respect and understand them.

Unlike Jimmy and Beth, Dorothy doesn't believe she or her feelings are worthless. But she is unable to trust the support of other caring adults. Dorothy encourages others to express their needs but is incapable of expressing her own needs. She can't ask for help; she feels threatened by the thought that she might need another person. If she does work up the courage to try to ask for help or to describe her feelings, she has trouble saying what she means.

Dorothy remembers that as a child she was much more trusting and was able to ask adults to help her.

"Even though I knew my mother didn't choose to be a mother, that my birth was an accident, I did feel I could ask her for things. She was really a career woman, and I was nothing but an inconvenience to her. I always knew that if it weren't for me, she would be doing what she really wanted to do. I felt a little guilty even asking for things like lunch, but I could do it.

"About the same time my mother had me, my aunt had an illegitimate baby. That baby was put up for adoption, but of course my aunt always remembered that I was the same age as her baby. She used to resent me terribly, and she used to try to kill me. I remember waking up several times with pillows over my face while she was trying to smother me. And *I* felt guilty about that. I felt guilty that I was the same age as her daughter. I kept saying to her that I was sorry. It didn't make sense, I know, but I said it over and over. Somehow I thought it was my fault she felt like that and wanted to kill me. I wondered if she was right and I should be dead. If I were dead, mother would have her career and my aunt wouldn't be reminded of her baby. But I didn't want to die, and so then I felt guilty that I didn't want to die.

44

"My aunt had a farm where my parents would leave me with her for the weekend or for a week while they were traveling or just wanting to be alone. I hated it there. There were so many bad things that happened there. I remember a few of them particularly.

"I was afraid of the pigs she kept. One time I told her that I was afraid of them. Quick as could be, she picked me up and put me in the pigpen. Then she took a big stick and ran it along the fence until the pigs saw me, came over, and started to chase me. They were mean and vicious, gross and ugly. They chased me from one end of the pen to the other, back and forth. I was screaming—they were screaming. It was slippery and muddy, and every minute I was sure I was going to fall and they were going to be all over me. By the time she let me out, I was hysterical from fright and exhaustion. She did this lots of times once she found out how scared I was of them.

"And one night I was nervous about a big spider that was near my bed. Field spiders can get pretty big, as big as a man's hand, and this was a very big one. I wasn't afraid of spiders, especially outside, but I didn't want that spider biting me during the night. So I asked my aunt to move the spider outside for me before I went to sleep. She didn't do this. Instead she went outside and got three more spiders. She brought them in, and she tied me down to the bed, and she put all four spiders on me. They crawled all over me all night, and they all bit me.

"Today spiders in the house or even bugs really freak me out. I can't stand them. They really get to me."

Dorothy's aunt taught her well, for Dorothy learned never to ask for help. She learned that when she told someone what she was afraid of, that very fear would be used against her. She learned that asking for help was the same as asking to be tormented, and that telling someone her problems or fears only gave that person a weapon to use against her. With a background consistently filled with betrayal and hurt, it was understandably difficult for Dorothy to accept a trusting relationship. Today, she is having to unlearn much of what she was taught as a child.

Unlike Dorothy, Amy is able to quickly form close relationships with other adults. She also feels that she is a friend to her children, and she expects their friendship in return. When they don't feel like being her friend, or when they actually say that they don't like her or even that they hate her, she loses control and hits them until they are "better" and don't hate her any longer. When they don't pay attention to her, this is also "proof" to Amy that her children don't like her, and she feels that she must change their behavior in the only way she knows—by abusing them.

Amy doesn't have any trouble forming intimate or trusting relationships with others, but she does have difficulty maintaining or deepening those relationships. While she is capable of being emotionally close to a person for a while, she soon puts up her defenses and retreats. Amy switches friends often, picking up new ones or renewing friendships with people she has deserted in the past. But she cannot continue in a deep relationship for a long period of time. Amy's past explains the impermanence she imposes on her present support system. One of her deepest fears, learned as a child and retained as an adult, is that she will be left alone.

"I was always afraid my mother would leave me. She always threatened it. She did it, too.

"I don't think she was gone for too long a time—maybe all day—but not for weeks or anything like that. It just seemed that every time I needed her, she'd leave.

"I'd try to pretend I didn't need her. When I didn't care whether she was there or not, she'd stay. So I'd try to pretend I didn't care. And I tried not to care, but sometimes, like when I was sick, it didn't work. Or when I was upset or something, I'd try to be near her. I wouldn't ask her for anything. I'd just stand by her. All I wanted was to be near her, just to be close to her. But she'd take a look at me, and she could tell. She could always tell. She'd shout at me, 'Don't look at me that way. Don't give me that sad-eyed look. I'm leaving you and never coming back. Don't you dare look at me that way.'

"One time I remember really needing her. I was eleven, and I had gone to a school play. My friend's father had dropped me off at the end of our block. It was a one-way street, so it was hard for him to take me right up to my house. So he dropped me off there. I was walking home when a man caught me. I thought then that he'd raped me, but actually he'd only rubbed his penis against my stomach and then let me go. I went home. I was sure I was pregnant, had V.D., and would probably die.

"I cried all night long wishing I could wake up Mom, but she never let me wake her up. In the morning she came in to wake me up. I must have looked pretty awful because she asked me what was wrong. I was so relieved—she'd never asked me that before. I was so afraid she'd leave before I could get a chance to say it. I shouted, 'Oh, Mom, I was raped last night!'

"She looked at me for a second, and then she said, 'You slut!' That's all she said. She turned and walked out. I didn't see her for three days and we never mentioned it again.

"Of course, I wasn't pregnant, I didn't get V.D., and I didn't die."

That's what Amy's childhood was like; she lived constantly with the fear of being left alone. Amy has generalized from her childhood relationship with her mother until now she believes that everyone will desert her. To protect herself from that possibility, she doesn't get close to anyone. Instead, she withdraws emotionally.

Pam *can* trust other people, but she still leans heavily on the role she played as a child. This role is real to her; she knows no other way to act. Yet she feels terrible about the way she treats her small sons.

"See what a bad mother I am? I never even feed them. It's 11:00, almost lunchtime, and they haven't even had breakfast. I never gave them dinner last night at all. See how bad I am? I don't do anything good at all around here. And I slap the children too, right on the face I slap them. I'm so bad.

"When my husband gets home, I'm going to have to tell him all the things I did today that were bad. I didn't make the bed. I didn't do the laundry. I don't blame him for being mad at me. What I do is wrong.

"I deserve what I'm going to get from my husband. I deserve my beating. Sometimes he really hurts me, but I deserve it. I shouldn't hit the children. I deserve whatever he does to me. I have no right to hurt his children.

"When my husband gets home, I'm going to get punished. He'll know I didn't do my jobs, and he'll punish me. That's right, he'll do the right thing. It's not right what I do. I'm a terrible mother. I have to remember to tell him I didn't go to the store today. He'll be very mad at me."

Pam is perpetuating her childhood cycle. Whenever she did anything wrong as a child, she was physically punished. She thought she deserved it. After her parents had finished punishing Pam for whatever wrong she had done, they forgave her. She "earned" her forgiveness by being abused. Pam was beaten almost every day of her life; afterwards, her parents would tell her that everything was fine and that they loved her. Everyone was happy again until the next day and the next beating. Today, Pam remembers that she felt better and cleaner after being punished than she did at any other time in her life.

As an adult, Pam is trying to recreate that feeling of being "good" and "happy." She wants to feel "clean," and there's only one way she knows how to achieve that feeling. So she works to see that she has a long list of wrongs to present to her husband each night when he comes home. She dutifully recites each item, and he just as dutifully punishes her for all the bad things she's done that day. The children are the only ones who don't feel "good" after a crime, punishment, and reward cycle.

Past experiences can also influence one's perceptions about the present and the future. Patty Jo had discussed her abuse problem with PA members, and she realized that abuse is a cycle, but she couldn't remember her own past. She couldn't understand where she had learned the destructive patterns she seemed to know so well, if indeed she had learned them at all. She frequently and violently lost her temper with one of her children and feared the depth of her anger. She wasn't conscious of anything bad in her background, though. She could remember fights and a few arguments, but no physical abuse, nothing to explain her own behavior. She felt that if she could only remember, if she could only learn how or why or where she had learned to be abusive, then she could better deal with her own abusive behavior. She thought she might have a chance then. One night, Patty Jo remembered.

"Right after I went to bed, I fell into a light sleep and for some reason started remembering my childhood. The first thing that came to my mind was so painful it woke me up, but I kept on remembering. All at once, I could see my parents in front of me, I could hear what they were saying to me. They were hitting me and yelling and hitting me some more—it went on and on. Then suddenly I knew why my right arm hurts me sometimes—it's because my parents threw me up against the living room wall and my arm got broken. It's because they beat me that my neck hurts, and my hip. I wonder why my jaw doesn't bother me more—they broke that, too."

Patty Jo had buried these childhood memories so deeply that she had no defenses against them. She reexperienced them as fully that night when she was thirty years old as she had when she was two and three and four and nine years old. She even experienced the physical pain of these abusive incidents; she actually walked stiffly for the next three days. She also relived the shame and horror of her past. Her most overwhelming feeling as the darkness of the night began to recede was one of shame—deep, personal shame. She had been so bad that her parents had had to do all of those things to her. She was convinced that it must have been her fault that her parents had treated her so abusively.

As the accumulated agony of the night began to wear her down, Patty Jo grew afraid for her own sanity. She thought that she couldn't bear much more, and she was afraid to tell her husband. He was the one person she didn't want to know about how unloveable she was. If he knew, he wouldn't love her either. He would leave her. Her deep feelings of personal unworthiness made it almost impossible for her to reveal anything at all about herself. She was convinced that she was unacceptable.

When Patty Jo first came to Parents Anonymous, she covered her face each time she spoke. She kept her head down and her hands over her mouth even when she laughed. She tried to hide any display of emotion. The first time she shared a negative feeling with us, she covered her face with one hand and rubbed the back of her neck with the other. Her body tensed as she waited for the group's reaction, and when nothing happened, when no one attacked her, she took her hands down from her face and began to rub her elbows and her forearms in a gesture which would become very familiar to us.

She always expected the worst, and since a good part of her life had been spent receiving the worst, her expectations made sense. They were legitimate expectations, but now she has to change them in order to adjust to her new world.

The child abusers met in this chapter are reliving their own past experiences through their children. They have a hard time responding lovingly to their children because they never received loving responses when they were children themselves. Like Beth, Jimmy, and Patty Jo, they need assurance that they are okay, that they are loveable. Like Dorothy, they need people to trust. Like Amy, they need support groups they can rely on. Like Pam and Peggy, they need to break away from the debilitating influence of the past and accept new roles.

All of the men and women encountered in this chapter have reached out for help. They are succeeding in breaking their cycles of child abuse.

Chapter 5
Stress and Abuse

Experiencing stress is not an option in life, it is a certainty. Stress affects various people in different ways, but each one of us is affected to some extent. When we ask people how stress affects them and how they deal with it, their answers are as varied as the following:

"I scream at my kids. God, do I scream at the kids."

"I have to go off by myself somewhere."

"Three drinks a day, two before dinner and one after. That's the way I unwind."

"Well, I have ulcers, but I'm not too proud of it."

"Poetry. I write poetry."

"I cry."

"I blow up and fight with my husband."

"Every Friday I get stoned. I count on it. I plan on it."

"I travel."

"I take it out on the kids."

"I get migraine headaches so badly I have to go to bed."

"I pick at my wife until she explodes, and then I fight with her."

"Hot fudge sundaes with lots of whipped cream on top."

Most people cope with stress according to learned patterns. We usually copy or model the same techniques that our parents used. If our parents dealt with stress in a positive way—by writing or talking or weeding the garden or cleaning the house, for example—we have a better chance of being able to do the same ourselves.

If our parents yelled at us when they were under a lot of pressure, however, chances are that we will yell at our children when we are under a lot of pressure. If our parents got sick when things got tough, we get sick when we try to cope with tough times in our lives. If our parents physically abused us, we are likely to batter our own children. It's easier and more familiar to do the same things we saw our parents doing.

Some responses to stress harm the person experiencing the stress but do not directly harm others. This group of responses includes migraine headaches, ulcers, high blood pressure, and complexion problems. These responses aren't creative or positive, but they don't have tangibly tragic results for other people either.

Many people who learned very poor coping mechanisms as children blow up under stress and explode at other people. Because their parents blew up at them, they now see blowing up at other people as the only option in a stressful situation. These people greatly fear stress for obvious reasons: they know that when they blow up, their children get hurt—and that is fearful.

People experience stress as coming from both the outside world and from inside themselves. The external stresses of the outside world—births and deaths, divorces, lay-offs, new jobs, sick children—exist independently of a person's feelings about them. Events like these occur in all of our lives, and we have little power over many of them.

Unavoidable stress also results because people live in particular places at particular times. Societal stress goes hand in hand with employment, unemployment, safety concerns, wars, foster homes, poverty, taxes, and all the other complications that go along with life in this country at this time. Big government, big corporations, and bureaucratic organizations seem monolithic, beyond our ability to effect change. Yet, as a group, we share the responsibility for the societal stress which accompanies the bigness of our nation. We are collectively involved and collectively responsible. We can, as a people, do something about the pressures that are part of our lifestyle.

Internal stress—that which originates within us—is partly made up of the "shoulds" and the "oughts," our own personal list of all we should and/or should not be doing. Feelings are the source of most internal stress, and they are strongly affected by the invisible baggage of past teachings and learnings. Most of us have the questionable ability to take on mild external stress and turn it into a major internal crisis. The loss of a job can become earth-shattering to a person who believes that "men always work at one job all their lives." The birth of a fifth child to a mother who believes it's "indecent to have more than four children" can catapult her into a crushing sense of worthlessness.

Internal stress is also fostered by past emotional experiences. An ordinary situation such as a house cleaning can be traumatic if beatings and tears always accompanied it in the past. Even the smell of furniture polish or window cleaner may suffice to resurrect past pain.

As children, both Chuck and Linda went on long car trips with their families. Their grandparents lived in other cities, and they visited them often. Both Chuck and Linda came from abusive backgrounds, and the stress of a car trip inevitably provoked abuse. A car is a high risk place for both Chuck and

Linda because of their past experiences. Chuck readily admitted that he had a problem in this area.

"It used to be every now and then, it didn't take long, it wasn't too bad, it went away as fast as it came. Each time I hoped it'd never be back.

"One time I was driving in the car with my son when I had this overwhelming urge to hit him. I pulled over to the side of the road, and I hit him for about five minutes. Then I started up the car again like nothing had happened and I was back on the road again before I really figured out what had happened.

"I drove us both straight to the hospital that time. No more chances for us, we've taken too many already."

On the day that Linda realized that a car was a high risk place for her and her children, she didn't even pull over.

"They'd been acting up in the back seat again. I told them over and over not to do that, but they did, they always did. This one time I put my hand over the back to try to make them sit down, and when I touched them, I just started hitting. The feel of their flesh started it. I hit and I hit, anywhere, everywhere, just hit and hit. I kept doing it until the underside of my arm was all sore from hitting the back of the front seat I was reaching over.

"Ordinarily I'm a very careful driver. Now I'm afraid to get back in the car with them. It might happen again; I think it *will* happen again."

A certain type of situation in and of itself will not determine whether or not stress will be produced or experienced. Rather, an individual person's *perception* of the situation will determine the amount of stress it contains. If a person perceives an event as stressful, it will be, and a crisis will take place inside that person.

Internal stress provoked Rose's crisis; her stress increased because of Rose's perception of the depth of her husband's anger. When a series of seemingly small events touched off her own sense of worthlessness, she inevitably lashed out.

"It was awful. I've gone and done it again. I've blown it. I said I'd never hit him again, damn it, and I did. Oh, I did. I really thought I was finished with that, but I'm not. Now he'll have an asthma attack this afternoon. Why did I have to do it again? He wasn't even being all that bad. He was just fiddling around, and then he started to get bad.

"Poor Jackie. It wasn't his fault; it never is. Will my

children ever be safe from their own mother? What a shitty situation!

"It's all my fault. I know it is. Everything is. It's my fault that Jackie has asthma. It's my fault that this happened with Art. He was yelling at me because the house wasn't clean enough. He wants me to do everything—all the laundry, the cooking, the yard work, the shopping—everything. He said it looked like I didn't even care anymore, like I was just trying to get him mad. And you know, Art doesn't usually have much of a temper. He hardly ever says anything like that. He's so quiet and easygoing most of the time. I'm glad, too. I can't take it when he yells at me. He doesn't yell loud, but when he gets even a mean tone of voice, I can't handle it. I sort of start into my slump. I get lower and lower and littler and littler in my chair until I'm just a lump. Then I can't see very well. The edges of things go all blurry. I can't see most of the room and then I can't see at all. I cry. Tears run down my face, quiet tears, and Art can't stand that. I guess that's what drives him crazy, at least afterwards he says it is. He leaves when I do that. He says he doesn't know what else to do. He tried to hold me once, and I nearly went crazy when he touched me, so he doesn't do that anymore.

"Then once he's gone I get feeling a little bit better, and I start seeing things clearly again. And then that's when I start to get mad, when I'm getting better. I get mad first at Art for making me feel that way. Then I get mad, a whole lot madder, at my dad. He was the one who started it all. He was the one who really did me in. I think it's because of the memory of him screaming at me and what always came next that makes me such a wreck with Art. Then I get mad at me, maddest of all at myself because I'm such an ass. Art is the nicest guy around, but I'm an ass. I really am. I get furious at myself. And that's when I hit the kids. Boy, do I hit them—especially Jackie. I really want to hurt *myself*, so maybe I hurt the thing that is closest to me, my kids. Usually it's Jackie. He reacts just the same way I do. Whenever I start yelling at him, he gets all slumpy and starts in with his tears. That's no way to react. I want him to stand up for himself. I don't want him to be like I am. I don't want to turn him into the cripple I am. I want him to learn another way to act. He makes me so mad when he gets so slumpy that I want to kill him. I want to beat it out of him. I want to beat *me* out of him. I want to beat me out of *me*, so I do it to him. What kind of a mess am I?"

To a casual observer, external things—outside of her

relationship with Jackie—seem to be going well for Rose. Her husband has a good job and seems to love his family; they own their own home; their children are healthy. But to Rose, things are not quite that simple. Because of Rose's childhood, scenes that might seem mild and inoffensive to other people are incredibly threatening to her. The slightest cross word carries her back into her past where she is once again powerless against her father's rage. As Rose reacts to her past feelings, her own present rage wells up and over until she beats her own children, especially Jackie. Rose's internal perception of her quarrels with her husband is very different from the external reality of what actually takes place, but that doesn't matter. The crisis is no less a crisis, the abuse no less harmful.

Penny was unable to handle the arrival of a sixth child. Her emotional response to all her children was impaired by the stress of having a new baby in the house. She came to PA for help, and after months of work, she related the changes she had been going through.

"I was the best-programmed robot you ever saw. I didn't think; I didn't feel. I was just dead inside, non-feeling. I didn't get happy or sad or mad or anything. I didn't want to make love or talk or fight.

"It wasn't as hard as it sounds either. We have six kids, and so I had plenty to do to keep me busy. I didn't have a lot of free time. In fact, I didn't have any. So if a thought would ever come into my head, I'd just push it down and bury it. *No, you can't do anything about that, forget it, lady, forget it all.*

"I never said no. I never refused to do anything for anyone. I did whatever they said—Peter, the kids, anyone— whatever they said. I was just there to be ordered around. I didn't think it even bothered me. I didn't get angry at them.

"I hadn't wanted the last three kids we had. I knew after the first three that I had my hands full. Actually even the third one was a surprise, but I didn't mind that one too much. Then I had an IUD put in, and I got pregnant with it and had another baby. So I got another kind of IUD, and then I had another baby. I finally figured, why want anything? What the hell, it didn't matter what I wanted anyway, so why not just forget it, forget all about me and just exist any way I could.

"Oh, Peter would get to me every now and then. But I'd catch myself and I'd say to myself, *Watch it, lady, what are you doing anyway? What do you think you're going to do with all these kids?*

Better just forget it. So I'd go and do something else. That was easy. There was always something that needed doing, something I had to do.

"It didn't make any difference anyway. I just wanted to get through the days as quietly as possible. No fuss, no trauma, no fighting, no shouting, no nothing—invisible if possible. Don't make trouble. That's all anyone wanted, including me. Take care of Peter, the kids, and the house. That's all he wanted. Shut up and do it.

"I guess I must have smiled every now and then. I know I laughed and it always surprised me because nothing seemed funny to me for years. I hated the sound of my laugh. It made my skin crawl. When I'd hear myself laugh that non-funny, creepy laugh it was awful for me. I just plodded through my days. It was safe and that was all I cared about—just get through it.

"Then it happened. One day everything blew apart at once. I lost my temper at my second son. I got really mad, and I hurt him. I had no idea I was going to do it, but I did. One minute I was getting a little upset with him, and the next minute I was hurting him, really hurting him. I really hurt him bad. He had to go to the hospital for a long time. I could have killed him. My grandmother always said my father could kill. I'm afraid I could kill, too. I think I've always been afraid of that. The safest thing seemed to be for me just to hold it all down, not to allow myself to feel anything.

"But it didn't work. All those things were still there, still bothering me even if I wouldn't admit it. I was afraid to face my own childhood and the pain I had had as a kid. I was afraid to think of my real feelings about my husband and about all the kids. I was afraid of my feelings. As it turned out, I had good reason to be afraid of my feelings. I thought I couldn't handle them, and I was right. I couldn't.

"It's taken me a long time to get comfortable with feelings, any feelings at all. It's hurt, but I haven't gone crazy. That's one of the main things I was scared of: I thought that if I let my feelings out, I'd go crazy, I'd just fly apart.

"Now I've discovered a lot of joy and a lot of pain that I didn't know existed. It's really safer now—now that my feelings aren't so bottled up—and it's a lot more fun. I'm still afraid of my anger—afraid I might not be able to control it, afraid that I might hurt someone again. Now when I feel my anger start to rise, I call for help right away. I reach for that telephone in plenty of time. And I'm in time now; I'm noticing how I feel. That's a big change for me, to know how I feel.

"I even surprise myself now and then. I'm getting to be funny. Even I think I'm funny and I laugh, really laugh now. The other day my husband was telling me how dumb and how stupid I was for doing something I had done. He was right—it had been kind of dumb. But he had been telling me about it for nine whole days, and that was long enough. I had had enough of it that time.

"So the next time he said it, I looked him right in the eye and I said, 'Yeah, but I'll bet I'm the best piece of ass you've ever had.'

"He just stopped dead with what he was saying, and he looked down at the floor. I was awful nervous that he was going to say something mean to me. He looked up at me, and kind of smiled a little. 'Yeah, matter-of-fact, you are,' he said.

"Can you believe it? It was fantastic!"

Penny's emotional deadness is well in her past now. Her fear of her feelings and of how she will react to them is lessening day by day as she learns that she can cope. Her emotional life has focused and grown in its own positive and authentic rhythm. She has learned how to deal with the stress created by the normal activities of six children and a husband.

Jane also experienced the external stress of having a new baby in the house. This stress was made even more complicated for Jane by the ambivalent lists of shoulds and oughts she had collected during her life and by the fact that she wanted to be a career woman and instead was stuck at home with two children. Jane's voice over the phone was strident; she talked fast without seeming to hear the ambivalence of her feelings or to understand the implications of her conclusions.

"I don't have a problem with abuse. Frankly, the very word makes me sick. I'm calling because of my daughter. She was a model child up until four months ago. For two and a half years she was a model child. Since then—that's when the new baby was born—she's been absolutely awful. The baby has been a nightmare himself ever since we brought him home from the hospital. He cries all the time, is allergic to milk, and is sick all the time. That's one thing I really can't stand. I can't handle it when anyone is sick; it really wipes me right out.

"I can truly say that since I've had that baby, it's been hell, sheer utter hell. It's been four months of misery. I didn't even want a boy, I knew it was going to be awful.

"But it's Polly who's driving me nuts. Not that I abuse her, I don't. I tell her I'll twist her lips if she isn't quiet, but I won't. At least I don't think I will. But I can't stand her right now. I can't even speak to her in a normal tone of voice. My husband says I scream at her all the time, and I do.

"It's not abuse. I don't hit her. I just hate her. It's normal though, I think. Every parent goes through times of not liking their kid. I wonder when I'll get out of this one. I never do anything to her. Oh, I've thrown her on the bed a few times, maybe a little too hard, but that's all.

"I feel confused a lot of the time. My mother says I think too much. She's probably right. She usually is. She's a very wise woman. She always knows just what to do. Sometimes she tells me to do things that I think won't work for me, and I feel guilty for even thinking that they might not work for me. It's my fault they won't work. The ideas are right. It's me who's wrong. They would work. It's me who won't or can't. But she can't live my life for me, I know that. I'm sure this is normal. I'm not any worse off than anyone else.

"It's the kids. I was a perfectly normal person before I had them and look at me now. I'm a wreck. But the kids are only young once, and I want to enjoy them while they're young. This is the time to be with them. Then I can go back to work. I'm going to enjoy this time, if it doesn't kill me, that is. They'll grow up, at least I hope they'll grow up. It seems like they never will. I do love them, and I want to raise them. But I wish I could do it part time. They aren't bad—at least no worse than other kids—but they *are* a handful. I wouldn't give them up for anything. I don't think I would, anyway."

Jane is articulate, intelligent, witty, and confused. The stress in her life is tangible—a new baby, jealousy from a three year old, a desire to please her mother, a desire to be a good mother, and a dislike of the responsibilities of parenthood. She can't cope, so verbal abuse has begun, and physical abuse could quickly follow.

David's experience of stress led him to find PA guilty for failing to change a situation which beat him down. His voice was angry over the telephone.

"Yeah, I beat my kid. Damn it, though, I didn't mean to. I was pissed off at him, but it ain't no big deal. For Christ's sake, the kid just spilled his cereal. I mean, it's no big deal. I made it as big as the whole goddamned world. I'm really pissed off at the whole goddamned world, and you, too, lady, you, too. It's partly your fault. You live here. You live in this fucking world; it's your fault, too.

"I'll tell you about it. I lost my job about two years ago. Company shut down, said they didn't make enough money or something. So I get canned. I worked there for fifteen years; my buddies thought I was nuts. They never gave me no raises, no nothin'. I never asked for nothin' because I thought they'd fire me if I did. So I worked there, that's all. It was a job.

"And then after I lost it, we run out of money quick. We never saved much, and pretty soon we were out. We got unemployment for a while, but then it run out and we was worse off than before. We had to go on welfare. My wife said our parents paid plenty into it and we had it coming to us. We were just taking now from what they put in, and we put in plenty ourselves and were just getting some back. But those days down there signing this and that and being shoved around was pretty shitty, let me tell you.

"Then we had to go into public housing because there was no way we could afford anywhere to live with the little bit of money they gave us. And then it got so we couldn't afford nothing, I mean not even food part of the time. It's awful every day, never enough money, never enough anything, never a job, never anything.

"And then one day I was really pissed, and the kid acts up, and I belt him one. Then I belt him again and again. I can't stop belting him; I just go on and on and on. You know I never hit that kid before in my life? I don't like hitting. I don't believe in hitting; especially, I don't believe in hitting kids, and especially not *my* kid. But there I was, and that's part of why I'm pissed at you. Because it's part your fault. You live in this world, you let this kind of thing happen. I never laid a hand on that kid before, when I was working and all. But now I'm in a bad way, I tell you, a bad way, and it's part your fault."

David's right. We do live in this world and, therefore, we are partly to blame. We aren't as diligent as we should be in guarding human rights. We all know enough ways in which people are abused to keep us busy for a lifetime changing the wrongs we see. For the sake of the children and for the sake of the adults who live with and raise the children, we must try to be more diligent.

We must also be diligent for the sake of the children who are themselves trying to raise children. Octavia is a fifteen year old who has a two-year-old daughter and an eight-month-old son. She was thirteen when she delivered her first baby; twelve when she got pregnant. The night she first called PA she was crying so hard she could scarcely talk. She said she couldn't control her temper with her children and found herself beating them too often. She had had trouble with her two year old that day; the little girl had gotten to her. Octavia wanted specific help in learning how to control herself.

There seemed to be more to the call than what Octavia was willing to express though. Her feelings didn't change during the conversation; nothing seemed to be resolved. Too much was left unexplained. Octavia even refused to give her phone number. She wanted help, but she was worried that it might come in an unexpected way. She didn't want any police showing up to take her children away from her, so she was afraid to risk telling PA anything specific about herself.

Later on that same evening, she called again. She had just abused her eight month old. It had all gone too fast for her, she said. She didn't know what had happened; she couldn't remember anything. She didn't know why it had happened or how or anything. She knew the baby had been crying and that he wouldn't drink his bottle. She said he didn't want his bottle of water, he wanted food; he was hungry, but she couldn't help that.

And then it started to make sense.

No, she hadn't eaten lately, she said. In fact, it had been three days, though it had only been two days for the children. They'd be all right, though; this had happened to them a lot, and they'd be all right. She knew there would be something to eat sometime. No, she had no family in town. Besides, they didn't even know she had had a second baby; they'd never seen the first one and wouldn't care anyway. No, there were no friends who could help her. But there *was* a dude coming over that night and he'd promised to bring her some money. It was almost midnight; he'd be there in an hour or two. She was a little nervous about his coming, though. The dude who'd come last night hadn't left any money after all, and he'd done some things to her that hurt her. She was a little sore tonight, but she needed the money and couldn't tell the dude not to come tonight.

Octavia has trouble controlling herself with her children, and it's understandable. What else can be expected of a fifteen-year-old, penniless, hungry, scared, lonely prostitute with two small children?

Stress, then, can be harmful—but it also can have some positive effects. The technique of dealing with stress in a constructive way can be learned. Most of the parents mentioned in this book didn't know how to use stress positively, but they're learning.

Maureen is one parent who can chortle when she talks about her learning experience. She had been in PA for about a year when her husband took a belt to their son.

"I didn't know I could stand up to him, to Deryl, my husband. I didn't even know I had the guts to try. But when he started to hit Joshua like that, I really went into action. I grabbed that kid away from him and I shouted, 'No. You're not going to hit him like that, I won't let you. And what's more, you're not going to hit me anymore either. You're not! No more hitting in this family.'

"That was really heavy for us. I never did anything like that before. I don't think I ever even mentioned that he hit me, and here I was laying down the rules about it. I meant it, too.

"Deryl said he was going to leave me, and so I said, 'Okay, good-bye.'

"He didn't go. He said that I shocked him so much that he thought I was cracking up and he'd better stay and take care of me. But I could have handled it if he'd gone. He said because I was such a bitch he wasn't going to give me any more money. I told him in that case I was going to get a job of my own. He laughed and mocked me. 'What can you do? You're no good. Nobody will give you money for anything you can do.'

"By this time I was so mad I didn't care. Even if the employers turned me down, they couldn't be as mean to me as he was, so what the heck. I went out and asked for a job and what do you know—I got it! Now I'll have some money of my own, but more than that, I discovered I have some stuff going for me that I didn't even know about. I'm not the pushover I used to be."

Stress is a form of energy and energy can be used positively. The parents in this book are learning how to channel that energy in creative, meaningful ways.

Chapter 6
Signs of Overwhelming Stress

The people whose stories are told in this book called PA because they felt that they either had abused or were in immediate danger of abusing their children. Because they were concerned about their children, they called for help. Most of these parents were unable to cope with the stress in their lives and the inability to cope led to abuse.

Behavioral changes are a good clue that a person is experiencing great stress with which he or she is unable to cope adequately and effectively. When her life became too much for her, Anne cried excessively. She couldn't understand her constant tears and knew that her tears left her vulnerable to the constantly recurring fits of screaming at her daughter.

"I just cry all the time. I don't understand. I'm not a crybaby, at least I never was before. I could handle things, certainly little things I handled just fine. But I'm not like that now. I can't even do the things I used to do so easily before. It's like I'm not even myself; I'm certainly not who I was before. I say things I never would have said. I'm so pitiful now. I don't like it at all. I don't like to be pitiful, and here I am crying right now while I tell you all this.

"My husband goes off to work in the morning, and when he leaves, I'm crying. He calls me during the day, and I start crying then. He comes home at night, and I cry again. I don't know how he stands it. I'm lucky to have a man who's so supportive. He really wants to help me, but he doesn't know how. I don't know how. I just cry.

"I don't have anything to be sad about, but that doesn't matter—nothing matters. It doesn't matter if I'm tired or hungry or mad or happy. It doesn't matter what my daughter is doing, what I'm doing. I just cry. No matter what, I cry.

"If people call me, I cry because they're bothering me. I don't think I can listen to anyone else's problems right now. I have enough of my own. If no one calls me, I cry because they don't like me enough to call. At least that's what I tell myself, but I guess I don't even believe *me* because no matter what happens, I cry. I cry and I cry and I cry."

When Anne was little and she cried, she was sent to her room. Her room was a haven, a safe place she could go to once she started to cry. Only very rarely would her parents continue to abuse her once she began to cry. She knew her tears were a disappointment to her father, and she didn't want to disappoint him, but she also knew that her tears guaranteed the ending of an abusive episode. Today she wishes she had the safety of a room to be sent to, and tears are still her most effective change agent. She knows no other way to affect her own life. Anne is literally crying for help.

Behavioral changes are one type of clue that stress is overwhelming someone and that abuse might be pending; another clue is a change in physical appearance or in general health. When stress piles up on Bev, she stops taking care of everyone and everything, including herself. Her physical appearance is a sign of how well or how poorly she's coping with her life.

"When I get nervous or uptight or frustrated or anything like that, I just don't function very well. The first thing I stop taking care of is me. I only get cared for when there's left-over energy. But I don't take good care of my house or my children either, or can't you tell? It's as if because they are part of me and it's okay not to take care of me, then it's okay not to take care of them either. Nothing that I have or that's any part of me is worth being taken care of, especially me. So the worse I feel, the worse I look and the worse my house looks and the worse my kids look. You always know what's going on inside of me by what's going on outside of me."

Some of the manifestations of stress in the body—such as ulcers, migraines, and asthma—are accepted as being closely connected to one's emotional well-being. In addition, stress can intensify physical illnesses, but physical illness itself can also be the cause of stress.

When Jill first came to PA, she had a great deal of stress in her life and a great many health complaints. She was less than five feet tall and weighed only sixty pounds. At one meeting, Jill sketched a vivid picture of her daily life.

"Every morning hurts; every day is painful. Pain is the first thing in the morning when I wake up, and it's the last thing at night before I go to sleep. When I wake up, I check in with my body to see where it especially hurts today. There isn't a place on or in my body that hasn't had something. My left side is worse than my right side. After my stroke, I was paralyzed on one side of my body for a while. I was only thirty-four when that happened. My right carotid artery is closed now and they say there's a chance the left one will close, too. But now I only limp, as you see, and have the use of one hand. It's not too bad any more, at least not compared to what it used to be.

"I was a 'change of life' baby and that was true in more ways than one. My father left me when I was a little girl and ran off with another woman. He divorced mother, left me, and married her. They've had kids of their own now, and he loves all of them. He never writes me or calls me or anything. Never. What the hell, though? I don't care, I don't need him. I don't need anybody.

"I don't need my husband, either. He thinks I need him, but I don't. I don't even know if I need Kevin. You know, I couldn't even have children myself; there isn't anything left. I had a hysterectomy when I was twenty-five and I couldn't ever have a baby. We adopted Kevin. We both wanted to have a child. Sometimes I can't remember why. No, I'm just kidding. We wanted him very much. We had to want him a lot to go through all that we had to go through. He has been raised by a lot of people other than me, though, and they've let him get away with murder.

"Now he expects a lot of things I won't give him. He doesn't mind as well as he would if I'd been in charge of him all the time, and he's mouthier than I'd like him to be. What a mouth that kid has on him!

"Now I have to get him back under control. Well, I can't do it, I tell you; I can't do it. I don't know whose kid he really is; so many people have raised him. It seems as if everyone in the world has had a chance to do it except me. I was so doped up for the first three years we had him, I don't even remember anything about it. I didn't know if I was coming or going. It's no wonder he doesn't act very loving to me. He hardly knows me. And it's no wonder I don't feel very loving about him. I hardly know him.

"I've been out of it as far as raising Kevin goes. It seems that the only thing I know how to do is to yell at him. I want to like him; I want to love him the right way, but I don't do that now. I don't want him to grow up feeling like I do. I want him to like himself and if I don't like him, who's going to? Where is he going to learn to like himself if I can't teach him?

"I haven't had a lot of practice being a mother. I feel so rotten that he hasn't had a full-time mother for his short life. But I can't help it. I didn't choose to get sick."

Today Jill is learning other ways to express her emotions and other ways to react to stress, but the trial and error process as she learns how to communicate with her body, her world, and her family is both time- and energy-consuming.

Under a great deal of stress, a person can almost lose the ability to appraise realistically the potentials in a situation and form logical expectations. This inability contributes to the development of an abuser because without being able to predict consequences accurately, people are continually disappointed, surprised, and caught off guard.

Trudie's unrealistic expectations are a clue to the observant person that she is in need of help and that there is too much stress in her life. Because she cannot deal with the present, she dreams of a rosy, perfect future. Trudie gets pregnant because she thinks that will make her life better. She expects pregnancy to solve all the problems she is having. She already has three little boys she can't manage—she can't feed them, dress them, or discipline them—and she is pregnant once again. She has no control over the children she has now (except when she is hitting them) or over anything else in her life. Although life is overwhelming for her, she admits to feeling good about being pregnant again.

"When I'm pregnant, people ask me how I am. Nobody ever asks me any other times. When I deliver a baby, I feel like I'm worth something, like I *am* somebody. I like to have people look at me and think I'm someone. And my husband treats me better when I'm pregnant. He doesn't make me do anything then. I like to sit on the couch, and when I'm pregnant, he lets me. He lets me do whatever I want. I like being pregnant, and I like being in the hospital. It's the only time in my life when I feel important."

Rarely do thoughts of the baby as an infant who will need care interfere with Trudie's enjoyment of her pregnancy. When her husband Dean found out she was pregnant, he tried to strangle her. She had told him she was taking the pill, but she wasn't. He is now distraught with anger, frustration, fear, and helplessness. Trudie is very happy as she sits on the couch feeling important and fulfilled. It is virtually certain that this new baby will become the fourth child to be abused in Trudie's and Dean's home unless some very serious changes are made before that baby is born.

The inability of some adults to predict the future realistically may be due in part to their inability as children to predict their parents' behavior. Neither Trudie nor Dean were ever able to formulate reasonable expectations for their parents' behavior. Their parents were sporadically violent, neglectful, or loving, depending on any number of variables over which their children had no control. Now that they are adults, Trudie and Dean must learn to analyze and evaluate their lives and to prepare themselves for times of stress.

How someone responds sexually can be another manifestation of an inability to deal well with the stresses of life. Carol experienced sexual trauma as a young girl, and coping with the stress of that past trauma is not easy for her. When Carol gets upset, she physically abuses her children more often and she wants to make love all the time.

Carol told PA about her feelings.

"I can't remember a time when I didn't know how to make love. Even in grade school, when all my friends were asking dumb, baby questions about sex, I was doing it. I knew all about it. When I started going out on dates, I did it all the time with them, too, except some nut who wanted to be a priest. I never said no to anyone, not ever. I didn't even try. I wouldn't have wanted to hurt their feelings and I know I would have if I had said no. I always thought everyone else's feelings were more important than mine. I still do. I like people and I want them to like me. So I always say yes.

"Everyone likes to make love, at least all men do. My father and grandfather used to do it to me a lot when I was little. They said it was because they loved me and that was how big people showed that they loved each other. I felt kind of good when my father said that. We were alone then; I was seven at the time, and he'd never wanted to be alone with me before. He wanted to be alone with me a lot after that, though. I had him all to myself then. It hurt, but I never got mad at him. It wasn't his fault. He didn't want to hurt me. He always asked me if he could do it. I said yes. If I said no, like I did once, it would hurt his feelings, and then he would start to cry and he would beg me. Then he would get mad and start to really hurt me. I don't want to talk about that part. So I said yes. It was easier and quicker that way and we both felt better.

"It didn't matter to my grandfather whether I said yes or no. He didn't care. But if I said yes, then I felt like I wasn't just a thing, that I was a person. He'd usually throw me down the stairs after he did it to me. He said I was a wicked spirit.

"Now my husband says I'm a nympho. He says I'd like him to make love to me for six or seven hours every day, and I would. That's true. But to be truthful, I don't think even that would satisfy me. I'm never satisfied. I always want more and more. I think about doing it with everyone: my friends, my family, my therapist, even my son. Everybody. All the time."

After working with the PA group, Carol has some ambivalence about the importance of her own feelings and desires. She is learning that her own personal feelings are just as important as other people's, but she is still uncomfortable about insisting on her right to be treated as she wishes. Because her wishes never influenced her early relationships, she didn't learn to respect them. Everyone seemed to feel perfectly free to use her whenever and however they wanted. She was raped repeatedly, by her father, grandfather, uncles, and cousins.

The pattern of repeated rape as a child has crippled Carol's ability to respond sexually as an adult. Orgasm for herself and her partner seems the only way to lov . Her identity as a sexual being is the only one she is comfortable with, and flirtation is the only way she knows to show her liking for someone else. Sexual attention is the only kind of attention she recognizes. The only time in her life when she feels "total acceptance" is during sexual intercourse.

The people in this chapter are not coping well with stress in a variety of ways, only one of which is the child abuse they feel they are involved in. How to cope with stress is a skill that they all need to learn.

Chapter 7
High-Risk Indicators
of Troubled Parenting

Many people who ultimately abuse their children give early signals that their parenting is in trouble. These signals are often connected to an attitude that predisposes a person to become abusive. For example, some parents feel overly responsible for their children; some parents have negative feelings about their children even before the children are born; some parents see themselves primarily in relationship to their own parents and only secondarily in relation to their children.

When a parent openly expresses concern or uncertainty about how to handle a child or a family situation, that is a clue that the parent is experiencing some internal turmoil concerning the child. It took five visits to the pediatrician before Marilyn felt courageous enough to be honest with him. She later told a PA group, "I finally said to him, 'I just don't know what to do with this kid. Really, he's so active I *don't* know what to do with him.'" Though Marilyn's remark to the doctor was neither violent nor dangerous in itself, it was indicative of a high-risk situation because it revealed Marilyn's feelings of inadequacy. She is unsure of herself and her abilities to parent her child. If her feelings of inadequacy are not relieved, she may become desperate, and abuse can easily follow.

Another subtle high-risk signal that abuse may be the next option for a parent is the statement that a child is a certain way because the parent has "made" the child that way. Laurie insisted, "It's because of me that Rachel cries too much. She always cries when her pants are wet, and that's because I changed her too often when she was a baby. I made her too sensitive. I changed her pants all the time, about thirty or thirty-five times a day. That's too much. It's my fault she cries now when she's wet." Laurie accepts responsibility for her baby's crying and for everything else the baby does. Laurie continues to accept and accept; she blames herself for each cry and each whimper until she can no longer tolerate the burden of her self-imposed responsibility. At times like those, she might well explode into abuse.

The attitudes parents express toward themselves and their children often signal high-risk relationships and situations. When parents feel bad about themselves, it's almost impossible for them to feel good about their children, and when they feel bad about their children, it's very difficult for them to parent well. It's sometimes very easy for a parent to express negative feelings about his or her children. Joe had thought and thought about his feelings but had kept them bottled up inside. When he started expressing them, Joe's attitude toward his son was a sign that he and his son were headed for an abusive episode.

"I hate that kid. That's really all there is to it. I hate him. I don't know what I'm going to do about it. I'm at the end of my rope. It's not that I'm such a bad father to him. I don't hit him; I let him do things; sometimes I even do things with him. But I hate him. I can't stand the way he looks, how he talks, the way he acts; I don't like anything about him.

"I was in the delivery room with my wife when he was born. He was born face up and so I could see his face even before he was all the way born. And I didn't like him even then. There was something about his face I didn't like. I thought maybe that was the way all new fathers felt, so I talked to some of my buddies. But they didn't seem to feel that way. I felt I was weird, like maybe I never should have been a father. I thought maybe I just hated kids.

"That didn't make sense. I used to like kids; I still like other kids. It's just this one I don't like. There's something about him.

"So I thought, well, then, I just don't like my own kids. I don't know why, but I know stranger things happen. I just have some kind of thing about my own kids. So I tried to talk my wife out of having any more. I thought with two kids around the house, it would be worse. And to tell the truth, I got so close to losing my temper with that first one I was afraid maybe I'd hurt someone some day. I'm still afraid.

"But it didn't do much good. My wife really wanted another baby. She didn't want him to be an only child. I finally said okay. I don't think she knew how it really was for me. I never told her that I hated him. I mean, how do you tell your wife you hate your kid, the kid she had? Who goes around saying he hates his kids? Nobody I know, and not me either! But I did hate him.

"So she got pregnant, and the whole time I was nervous. I didn't know how I was going to manage. I was worried about the new baby, the one coming into this family with a father who hated his own kids; and I was worried about how I was going to manage with the one we already had while she was in the hospital.

"I thought maybe I wouldn't go into the delivery room with her this time. I wondered if it was the birth bit that had turned me off or something like that. But she wanted me to be with her, and so I went. To tell the truth, I was a lot more scared than she was.

"This baby was born face up, too, and I watched its face come out. What a difference! I took one look at this baby, at this face, and I just melted. It was the most beautiful face I ever saw. I was so happy to feel that. I didn't even know if it was a boy or girl when I started feeling that good. I didn't even care which it was. I just knew it was the most beautiful baby in the world. It turned out to be a boy, but I didn't care. I would have loved him no matter what he'd been.

"And then you know what I hoped? I know it was stupid, but I hoped that I had finally learned how to love a child of mine. I hoped that I was going to go home and love that other boy of mine.

"So I went home, and I looked at him. And I hated him just as much as ever. I don't know what's going to happen to him. I do know he'd be better off with a dad who could love him than with me. It's too late for that now, though. I can be polite to him. I can tolerate him if I grit my teeth, but I think he's going to know someday. I'm so fussy about the new baby. How can he not know? I don't want him even near the baby.

"I don't know what we're going to do. I don't want my wife to know how I hate him. What if she starts hating him, too? I don't know how we're going to live with this. The poor kid. God, I can't stand him."

Eventually, Joe learned to analyze his feelings; he learned to recognize that the things he hated about his son were the very things he hated about himself. Initially, that realization didn't bring about any monumental change for Joe. But as he changed some things about himself that he didn't like—and as he accepted those things he couldn't change, such as his own physical appearance and that of his first child—Joe came to tolerate and then to appreciate his son.

Most parents are neither as aware of nor as articulate about their feelings as Joe was. In cases like these, danger signals may be found in discussions of difficult pregnancies or deliveries, hard babies to care for, illness during pregnancy, or divorce or death during pregnancy or during the infancy of the child.

Diane's memories of her pregnancy could have been a tip-off to anyone listening to her that there was a strong possibility that she would soon abuse her son.

"I knew before I had him, almost the minute I got pregnant, that I was in for it. The whole idea of being pregnant was disgusting to me. I was sick most of the time. It seemed like I got out of bed the minute I got pregnant and started throwing up. I saw more of the inside of the toilet bowl for the next three months than I did of anything else in the house. I know every crack in that toilet bowl, every little mark on it. I spent a lot of time staring at it feeling horrible. I sat on the floor for months, either throwing up, about to throw up, or recovering from having thrown up.

"Then once the baby got moving around inside of me, that was the end of my peace. It was even worse then; he never let me sleep. Every time I'd lie down to take a nap, he'd get started. He knew, I know he did. Even the doctor said he was a 'live wire'. He said he wished me lots of luck with him. And that kid has always been so stubborn. Even the doctor said it before he was born. He was turned the wrong way inside of me, and they had to turn him before he could be born. Every time they did, he flipped back again. Just one flip and there he was, back the wrong way. I know he did it on purpose.

"In the delivery room it was even worse. He gave me hell in there. It was terrible. I thought he was going to split me in two. I couldn't believe how much it hurt. I kept asking them to give me something for the pain, but they wouldn't. They made me suffer through it. They said it would be worth it. They were wrong. But finally he was born. That was my second mistake. My first was in getting pregnant; my second was in letting him get born. Once I got him home, it was the same thing. He did everything he could to cause me trouble. Cry, cry, fuss, fuss, that's all I hear from him. I don't know how much more trouble he has planned to make me miserable, but I'll bet it's plenty."

Babies don't willfully cause their parents trouble at birth, of course, and parents who perceive their babies doing this credit them with more than they deserve and therefore give them much less than they deserve. A baby whose entry into the world caused the mother so many problems may be met with ambivalent feelings from the mother, and a negative parent/child relationship may be the end result.

A parent who describes her or his baby as "different" is really saying that this baby is not what the parent either expected or wanted. The baby may be smarter, dumber, bigger, smaller, balder, hairier, better, or worse than expected; at any rate, the fact that the baby is perceived as "different" means that the parent has some adjusting to do.

A parent needs to make the transition from child to parent himself or herself before being able to parent effectively. The arrival of a baby doesn't automatically guarantee that that transition will occur. Elizabeth was still more of a daughter than she was a mother; her "Mommy" was more of a central figure in her thoughts than either her child or her husband.

"The only reason I stay married at all is because I don't want Mommy to say I'm a quitter. I can't stand my husband; I really can't. He's a bad person, and even worse than that, he's bad to the kids. I've called the police four different times because he was beating the kids or me. I keep telling him, 'Don't hit the babies,' but he hits them anyway. The older ones I don't mind so much, but the babies, that's bad. I tell him, 'At least don't hit them in the face.' I say, 'What d'ya want to do that for? Ya don't got to hit 'em in the face. They got plenty of butt to beat. Ya don't got to hit 'em in the face.' But he still does.

"My mom says it's good for us to get beat. You'd think she'd know better. She got it from my dad all the time. She didn't think it was so good then, but now she says it's good for us! I need it, she says, I always did. I don't know about needing it; but I always got it, that's for sure.

"She says I ought to stay with him. I know I can do it. For about the first time in my life, I know what she wants and I know I can do it for her. But why does she have to want me to do this? I want her to think I'm good, but why this way?

"It's so much easier when she talks to me about my son Bobby. I can do that part, I know she's right about him. And I do want to do it the way she says."

Patricia, too, wants to please her parents. She has been married for six years and has two children of her own, yet her parents come up in her conversations more often than do either her husband or her children. She cannot talk about her children without talking about her parents.

"My son's been crawling around on the floor all morning. He was having a good time. He just learned how to crawl, and he wanted to do it. But Mommy says he shouldn't be doing that. She wouldn't say that if it wasn't right. She knows what she's talking about. She's had four kids of her own, and she's raised us up pretty good.

"I guess Mommy's right, she usually is. I don't know why I'm even talking about it. I already put him back in the playpen, and I won't let him out again. I'm glad she told me."

The baby she was talking about was twelve months old. He not only enjoyed crawling around on the floor; he needed to in order to develop his independence and his skills. It seemed likely that he would stay in the playpen unless "Mommy" changed her mind, however—even though Patricia herself feels that the baby is happier out of the playpen. Instead of leading an adult life of her own, Patricia is trying to mother her children to please her own mother. She tries to do and say what she thinks "Mommy" would do and say. It's no surprise that when Patricia explodes, as she often does, violence follows.

Other people are as strongly tied and bound to their parents by intense dislike as Elizabeth and Patricia are to their parents by the desire to please. These people have similar incomplete relationships with their parents, but they are seeking revenge rather than the elusive love they once missed. Denise has been married for eleven years, has four children, and speaks of her father often. She wants revenge for his neglect of her as a child.

"I think about my father a lot more than he deserves, that's for sure. He really doesn't deserve anything at all from me, unless it's the hurt to pay back some of what I suffered from him as a kid. I think more about how I'd like to hurt him than anything else. I fantasize all kinds of situations where he wants me to do something, and I can say no. That feels good to me.

"I actually shouldn't be spending all this time thinking about him. I'm an architect and a mother and a wife. I need to concentrate, too. But all I think about is my father. It's like some kind of a tennis game going on in my head: his shot, my shot, foul, my serve, his slam, my point, his point."

Denise is sending out signals that she will abuse her children; it is likely that she will neglect them as her father neglected her. She is tied to her past, and her obsession with her role as a daughter is interfering with her functioning as a mother. Her attention is so focused on the past that her present behavior is inadequate. Whenever Denise as a child reached out to her father for help, he turned her away, and Denise is now doing to her children the same thing her father did to her. This destructive cycle is sowing its seeds of hurt and pain for future generations of children and parents.

Chapter 8
Times of Crisis

"It's like being caught in a cyclone. I can't do anything; the force of it is too strong. It almost goes on without me—even though I know I'm part of it. It's like *it* knows more than I do.

"And it's always the same: getting mad—blowing up—beating him—wanting to kill myself. It's always the same.

"I float on top of this big ocean; the waves are moving up and down; I don't do anything. I just float and hope I can hang on one more time."

There was a tragic rhythm about Maggie's abusive episodes. Her upsets, her abuse, and her resultant despair seemed to her to have a life and a will of their own. Even her suicidal wishes seemed less chosen than compelled, less initiated than imposed. She felt trapped in her abusive behavior and powerless against it.

Each abusive episode contains definite crisis points—times when the parent could conceivably change the pattern of abuse. For Maggie, there were some moments when she had more power to choose than others. Finding alternatives to abuse requires the ability to recognize those moments. It would seem that the most logical moment is right before abuse occurs; unfortunately, most parents must gain some new understanding before they are able to make full use of the choices present in this moment. Like the crest of the wave Maggie was talking about, the moment immediately preceding an abusive incident is often too strong, too emotional, and too powerful to deal with.

Another moment when a parent can choose how to handle a situation occurs right after he or she regains control of herself or himself. The parent must now decide what to do, and the list of alternatives usually isn't very long: commit suicide, run away, call for help, or try to forget the abuse and hope it won't happen again. This decision must be made within an abyss of shame, sorrow, pain, and regret.

An abusive encounter between parent and child seems to be more laden with heavy emotion than almost any other situation in life. Love and hate, fear and exhilaration, sorrow and anger are all strong, volatile feelings. They are natural feelings, but the natural response to them is by no means always positive. The habitual response of some people to any overwhelming set of feelings or circumstances is child abuse.

One of the first things PA encourages abusers to do is to begin to notice some of the danger signals that an abusive episode is pending. This signal might be dependent upon a certain set of circumstances—such as a particular time of the month related to either the menstrual cycle or the pay-day cycle or some bodily sensations.

By paying attention to her body and focusing on the messages it is sending her, Sue has learned to recognize a signal that abuse might happen.

"I can tell now when I'm close to abuse. Sometimes I can hold on for days and not do it, but usually it's not that long. Usually it happens sooner. I can tell by how the muscles in my hands feel when I'm getting close. I feel I'm clutching at life with my nails. My voice sounds kind of funny and squeaky to me—it's skinny and high—and noises get to sounding very loud to me. When I start to feel the noises on my skin, then I know I'm in trouble. It's like noise is heavy then. My arms get all tingly in the elbows, and my head feels like it's too tight. The top of my head feels like it's pushing down on the rest of my head and clamping it in. Then I'm scared all the time. I know something bad is going to happen, but I don't know how to prevent it. I know I'll explode, and when I do, Pammy is going to get hurt. I hang on as long as I can, but then I can't hang on any longer.

"Once I start, once it all starts to come out, I get this wonderful relaxed feeling. I feel so good. It feels so good to stop trying to hang on, to have everything flooding out of me. All that tension, all that tightness, out it flows. It just runs down my arms and out my fingers. It's such a relief. It feels so good until I see Pammy again and see what I've done to her. That's when I think I have to give up; that I'm not fit to live, I can't make it, and I'm nothing but an animal—no, not even that; worse than an animal."

Sue feels horrible after her abusive episodes, but *during* them, she is conscious of the good feeling which accompanies the release of pent-up energies.

Peggy also lets her feelings out explosively but she never enjoys being angry. She hates to be out of control; she hates to behave in ways that she wouldn't choose if she had a choice.

"I hate it; I hate every second of it. Being out of control is the worst thing in the world to me. I know when it's coming. I can tell ahead of time and I don't want to scream at them. I hate screaming. But that's what I do. I scream like a fishwife, and I can't help it. I don't know how to stop. It just overflows—I start and I don't stop until I'm hysterical. I finally collapse in

76

hysterics. What kind of mother is that? What kind of person is that?"

Many newly abusive parents cannot anticipate their explosions at first. Nancy admits that she hasn't learned to notice what's going on inside of her.

"I have no idea it's coming. One minute I'm calmly dusting or sleeping; then she comes in to ask me something or to say something to me or even just to be with me. I turn to speak to her or look at her, and the next thing I know I'm hitting her with a rag or a broom or whatever it is I've got in my hand. I don't know what happens to me. I know I didn't want her to come in. But one minute I'm fine, and the next minute I'm totally out of control. I'm scared all the time I'm with her. I'm scared every time I even think of her. What can be going on inside of me that I can change so fast and be so dangerous to her?

"I try to stay away from her as much as possible, to keep her in the other room or somewhere I can't hurt her. She won't cooperate though. You'd think she would, she's the one who gets hurt. I tell her, 'Mommy's not feeling very well today, and I don't know what I might do if you stay around me. Please go into the other room and stay there.' But it doesn't work. I don't understand. Sometimes it almost seems as if she's worse at times like that. She comes in and whines and carries on, and then it happens again."

Nancy's feeling that at any moment she might lash out at her daughter keeps her living in constant anxiety. Although she tells her daughter to stay away from her when she's uptight, that isn't always a real option to use with small children.

Learning to anticipate crisis times is the first thing that parents who want to stop abusing their children must do. Recognizing that their elbows or their stomachs or their heads signal trouble is the first step toward breaking the cycle of abuse. The second step is to call for help.

The first time a person calls PA, a crisis has usually occurred; the call usually comes after an abusive episode. These calls are tremendously sorrowful and painful. A parent has hurt a child, and the parent hurts, too. The parent is experiencing grief and remorse of gigantic proportions. At the same time, the parent may be reliving incidents from his or her own childhood. Louanne expressed the pain she felt after abusing her daughter.

"It's her face, her precious little face. When I look at that face and it's all crumpled up because I've hurt her, I just want to disappear. To think that I'm the one who made her look that way makes me want to die. But even that wouldn't do any good. I already hurt her. I love her more than anybody, more than me, more than the whole world, and I made her scared, scared of me, her own mother!

"I don't want her to be scared of me. I was always scared of my mother, and I don't want my little girl to be scared of me. I always said the one thing I would never do is make my little girl feel about me the way I feel about my mom.

"But that's exactly what I've done. I've made her scared of me. I want her to love me, not hate me. And she must hate me. *I* hate me for what I do to her! I love her so much, and I'm such a shit. I don't deserve her, and what would I do if they took her away from me? She's my whole life. She's the only one who loves me. I love her, and what do I do? I yell at her, and I hit her. It's not her fault. She's good; she's not a bad little girl. I'm the one who's bad. I always had a vicious temper.

"All I want is for her to grow up happy and safe and feeling good about herself. I want it to be good for her. I want her to be everything I'm not. And what am I doing? I'm making her grow up thinking she's no good, the same way I think I'm no good. You'd think that since I know so well what it feels like, I'd be the first one not to do it. And I would, too. But I just can't seem to help it."

For Louanne to reach out for help after hurting her child is an important step for her to take in stopping her abuse.

The person at the other end of the PA phone has a unique opportunity to be with abusive parents during what they consider to be their worst moments. How the PA worker reacts is of the utmost importance.

There's no need to minimize the tragedy of the abuse; abuse is always tragic. If instead, the parent is accepted and supported, chances are that the next time that parent loses control he or she will be able to call earlier. Ideally, such calls will come closer and closer to the actual incidents until they will precede them. When a parent reaches for a phone instead of abusing the child, it is a victory for everyone.

The call that comes before any abuse has occurred differs from the one that is made following an abusive incident. After abuse, the parent is filled with guilt and great sorrow. The parent who recognizes that abuse is near and who calls to forestall that painful episode displays the raw, wild, forceful emotions of anger, passion, and hate. The violent feelings are still within the parent but they have not yet been directed at the child, so the parent's voice is thick with the power of those restrained energies. Reflexes are quick and strong. This is not the time for thoughtful, gentle responses from the person at the other end of the line; it is not the time for analysis or intellectual activity. The response must meet the parent on the parent's own emotional level. The verbal exchange must be fast and powerful in itself. During the call, the parent must be able to release some of his or her pent-up feelings.

The following was an actual phone conversation between a furious parent and a PA telephone worker.

"I'm so mad I think I'm going to KILL that kid!"

"You sound really mad, Julie."

"You're damn right I am; I'm FURIOUS!"

"What do you feel like doing?"

"I want to scream at him; I want to yell at him. I'm afraid of what I want to do. I want to punch his stupid face in."

"What do you want to scream at him?"

"That I hate him; that he's a bastard—a no-good bastard."

"Okay. Let it go. Tell me. Pretend I'm him. Scream it all at me."

"I hate him. He's a no..."

"No, speak right to him. Tell him straight into this phone."

"I hate you, you little bastard. You drive me crazy. You do it on purpose. You want to drive me crazy. I want to throw you up against that wall so hard you'll never come down, and if you did, you'd be a puddle. I'd like you to be so far away from me that I would never, ever, EVER have to look at your stupid face, your stupid, ugly, hideous face, your stupid fat face! You're the worst kid in the whole world, and I can't stand you. Do you hear me? I hate you. I can't stand you. Will you please get out of my life forever?"

"Go on. More."

"I can't stand anything about you, especially the sight of your face. You're so much like my mother you even look like her. I hate her, and I hate you. Do you understand me? I hate you!"

"Do you have a pillow you can reach?"

"Yes."

"Punch that pillow now. Dig into it with your whole arm, both arms, all your strength. Yell at it and punch it and hit it."

"I'm going to pretend it's him."

"If you want to, do that. Just hit and hit it. Scream at it while you're hitting it. Say all those things all over again."

Julie put the phone down—not gently—and could be heard punching the pillow. After a few tense minutes, she returned to the phone.

"Speak to him some more now. Tell him some more," the PA telephone worker said.

"I'm still mad at you, but it's not all your fault. You can't help the way you look. You did almost drive me over the edge, but not quite. I'm glad that pillow wasn't you."

"Me, too. Congratulations! You did it! You get gold stars in your crown and rousing cheers. Now let's talk. What's been going on over there?"

When Julie had first called, her voice had been thick and angry. Other people's voices are thin, thready, tightly controlled. The force behind the voice may be so flattened that the person sounds only slightly angry. Gretchen's tentative reaching out for help was such a call.

"I'm very upset right now. Can you talk with me?"

"Yes, I can. How are you?" the PA worker asked.

"I need to talk. Or I need something. I feel like I need to cry, but I don't know how to cry. I need something, but I don't know what. I need to feel better. I'm upset right now."

"What's happened?"

"My son broke one of my best lamps. We don't have a lot of things, but what we do have is nice. I have nice things. I've worked hard to save the money for them, and they're nice. Now that we're moving, they're even more important. It's not as if that lamp could be replaced, either; it can't. It was made by a company that's gone out of business."

"No wonder you're upset. That's really a shame. How did it happen?"

"He broke it doing something he'd been told not to do. He was eating his sandwich at his little desk in front of the TV. I've told him he's not allowed to do that because he might trip over the cord and break the lamp. I've always been afraid of that, and today that's what happened."

"I guess you were right to be concerned about it. What did you do then? How did you react?"

"I sent him to his room."

"Good for you! Congratulations!"

"I knew we had to have some distance between us. I'm glad I saw that. But what am I going to do now? I have all these feelings inside of me, and I feel like I'm going to explode. I don't know how to get them out."

"What do you feel like doing? What would feel good to you?"

"Well, the one thing that would feel the best to me is the one thing I shouldn't do. The very thing I'm trying not to do is the only thing I want to do."

"Yes, and not only trying not to do; you're doing better than trying, you're making it. What else might feel good to you? Think of your own body. Where do you hurt? Where is it tense? What would feel good to you?"

"It would feel good to cut myself. I think if I could just cut myself and watch the blood flow out, I might feel better. If I could just cut myself deep..."

"Gretchen, that's not the one we're going to work with. How about hitting the pillow? Hold it up against the wall so you can feel the hardness of wall behind it and yell out loud while you punch it."

"I'll try, but it's not going to work. I have too much going on inside. That won't work, but I'll try."

She was gone for only a very few moments, and no noise was audible over the phone.

"Well, I'm back."

"You sound better, Gretchen. Did it help?"

"Yes, but not the way you think. I caught my nail on the wall as I was trying to hit the pillow. I tore the nail past the quick and it really hurt. The pain helped. I do feel better, but am I really better? Sometimes I think I'm better, and then I explode later on."

"When you explode later on, do you recognize your feelings and do something about them? Something like talking to someone and doing something physical?"

"No, I just control them. I keep myself calm."

"Then that's the difference, Gretchen. This time you've taken care of them. You've handled them, you're not ignoring them. You've paid attention to them and you've done something with them."

"How can you be sure I won't have trouble later on?"

"I can't be sure of that. I think you won't. But I *can* be sure you know how to use the telephone to call for help; you've proven that. So if you have the slightest bit of trouble or even if you're concerned that you might have trouble, just call back. I'll be glad to talk to you."

"But you know, I have to ask you this, what kind of person am I that I have to hurt a little child to make myself feel better?"

"For one thing, you're not that kind of person. Doing that kind of a thing to make yourself feel better doesn't mean you're that kind of person. It's all you ever knew how to do when you were angry, it's all you ever saw done in your home when your parents were angry. But now you're learning something different, something better. How are you feeling now, Gretchen?"

"I feel better, but I'm still scared. I've never felt this way before without hurting him."

"Don't you feel proud of yourself? You ought to. You've done something wonderful. You ought to be very proud of yourself."

"Well, yes, I guess maybe I am. Yes, I am proud of myself. I really am."

Both Julie and Gretchen had been able to call for help in the midst of crises. But as Gretchen said, a crisis doesn't happen only once. It may happen again minutes or hours later. The feelings bubbling and churning inside will eventually come out. The real question is one of *how* they will come out. Feelings may emerge in the old familiar way—the way of child abuse—or they may be released in a new and different and better way. But that new and better way has to be learned, just as the old way was learned. The new way of behaving doesn't come naturally. Old habits are hard to break.

Chapter 9
Choosing Alternatives to Abuse

Responding to crisis and trauma by taking one's feelings out on a child is a particularly hard habit to break. In most cases the parent has been conditioned to this type of response for as long as he or she has been alive. Grandparents and parents have all reacted the same way; for many generations, abuse has been the chief means of handling emotional stress.

The guilt, shame, and regret which result from child abuse become so strong that the abuse is stress-producing instead of stress-relieving. Many parents who recognize this look for other options. They decide not to abuse. The choice is never an easy one, although it is a clear one. Parents who decide to stop abusing must learn to recognize crisis times and must strive to understand why they abuse. But—most important—they must find new behavior patterns, new ways of coping with stress, new ways of relating to their families.

Jan, who has been coming to PA meetings for a year now, is slowly changing her behavior and choosing alternatives to abuse. She is divorced and lives with her two sons although she is not yet certain she will keep them, especially her older son, John. She alternates between wanting to give John up and wanting to keep him, for she has serious trouble with him. She knows, however, that if John weren't around, she'd have trouble with Jerry, her second son. In the past, Jan has felt incredibly powerless where John was concerned. In fact, she felt powerless in most areas of her life. Her children, her house, and even her own body all seem to make demands on her that she feels powerless to resist, powerless to refuse, and powerless to fulfill. When Jan first came to PA, she knew she didn't like the way things were in her life, but she perceived herself to be without any choice except the one she had learned as a child—and that pattern of behavior brought only pain. It didn't make her happy, but she knew nothing else.

Jan went to therapy for a year before she came to PA. Not even a year of therapy seemed to have helped much, though. Nothing was better. She understood more of what was going on—she knew more about the dynamics with her children, her friends, and herself. She had some good "head" knowledge, but that didn't help. She didn't know how to make decisions or choices; all that head knowledge didn't get translated into any safe and positive difference in her life. She knew that when her boyfriend, Ben, came over and fought with her, she was going to end up abusing John. Ben abused her children, too, but she didn't think she could safely stop him. When she did tell him that he couldn't come over because of the children, she resented the boys because she felt that they had forced her to choose them, and she ended up abusing them herself. Everyone said, "Give up Ben." But he was the only person in the world who said he loved her; he was the only one who called her up and said he wanted to be with her. How could she give that up? She couldn't—or rather, she wouldn't. Jan's emotions were ambivalent and contradictory, and they immobilized her. She hid her anger underneath all of the insights she had gained through therapy. But they always erupted when stress became too much to bear. Finally, she came to PA for help and support.

During her work with PA, Jan learned some alternatives to abuse. One day she hit a cupboard in rage. "Bravo!" the group said.

"But it didn't do any good," Jan responded. "It didn't work. I hit John even harder later on in the day. It didn't help at all."

"Yes, it did," they insisted. "It *was* different. You *did* break a pattern. You *did* do something other than hit him, at least at first. You now have an option. You now know how to do something other than hit John when you're angry."

Jan had succeeded in breaking a pattern. She had done something differently, she had experienced a different reaction. Her attitude hadn't changed, however. She called late one afternoon soon after that saying that she had decided to go back to "pounding" on John. "I can't take this disrespect," she said. "I can't stand it. The only way I can get any respect from him is to hit him, and so I'm going to go back to hitting him. It's worse around here than it ever was, and I'm not going to put up with it. I just want you to know I'm going back to pounding on him."

Jan was caught in the middle of change. She knew that she could avoid hitting John at least some of the time; she now knew how to. And now John knew that he wouldn't always get clobbered when he misbehaved. He was feeling a lot freer and behaving a lot worse. He, too, was caught in the middle of change. He didn't know what the new pattern of behavior was going to lead to, but he did know that things were unpredictable and new. Neither Jan nor John had at their fingertips a new set of behaviors to replace the old ones, so each encounter between them was, for a time, a new crisis. Like prize fighters, they had to circle each other, deciding who would do what first and what reaction would follow. They kept a mental score of who won and who lost. Neither could trust the new behavior, count on it, or predict the outcome. That was exhausting for them both. When they did fall back into an abusive incident, it was stronger and more violent than before. The familiarity and intensity of abuse were almost a relief compared to the strangeness of the new pattern they were designing. After each abusive incident, though, one or the other of them would go back to trying to live the new way.

In the old way, Jan's day had centered around her children. She got them up, cooked their breakfast, got their clothes and books and lunches ready for school, drove them to school, cooked for them, cleaned for them, flushed the toilet for them. She gave herself to them, and they always wanted more—more snacks, more driving, more TV, more toys, and more of her. And when she had no more to give, they got to witness her temper erupt. And John got abused.

During most of the day, Jan controlled her anger. She trapped it in fuzzy thinking and unclear decisions. Indecision and inconsistency scattered her feelings and made them seem less intense. Jan feared that if she ever experienced the full intensity of her feelings she might discover that she hated her children and wanted them far away, perhaps even dead.

Jan's children also had ambivalent feelings which caused them great stress. Jerry knew that his mother would be nicer to him if he hated John. After all, she hated John, and if he also hated John, then Jerry and his mother would be on the same side. But Jerry loved his brother, and he didn't know what to make of that. Should he deny it and lie about it or acknowledge his love and have his mother hate him, too? This was not an easy decision for a seven year old. One day, while entertaining himself with paper and crayons, Jerry wrote out his dilemma in capital letters on huge cards: *Jerry loves Mommy. . . Jerry cannot love John, too, can he?* As he laid down the last card, Jerry looked up and said, "Can I?"

"Yes, you can," he was told by the PA child care worker.

And so Jerry went on writing the rest of the sentence: *Jerry loves Mommy. . . Jerry cannot love John, too, can he? Yes, Jerry can love Mommy and John.* As he put down his cards, Jerry's face showed his relief even as it revealed a lingering ambivalence. He didn't know how to live out this new permission, but he did recognize the possibility for change.

For Jan, change meant needing some very clear and specific instructions. Her therapist had told her, "Don't wake them up in the mornings. Buy them alarm clocks and let them wake themselves up. Don't serve them food whenever they want. Put the meals on the table and leave them there for thirty minutes. Then take them away. Don't drive them to school when they miss the bus. Let them walk." He concluded, "You need to learn to become less involved with your children."

But what would this mean for Jan? She had had a full time job living for three people, and she had now turned over the responsibility for two of those lives to their rightful owners. What was she going to do now? Well, Jan got a job. At first, she was exhausted and guilty and scared that she couldn't do her work well. But she got used to working outside the home. She found that she could function well in the *real* world, wherever that is, and that her children could manage some things on their own. She announced to John and Jerry that she didn't think she would be the one to clean up their rooms anymore. If they wanted clean rooms, then they could clean them themselves. And they could also see to it that their dirty clothes went into the hamper if they wanted them washed. And if they didn't put their dirty clothes into the hamper and if one day they didn't have any clean clothes, well, she rather thought they could handle that any way they wanted, but that would be their problem to handle and not hers.

That's how Jan's attitude has changed. She doesn't have to hit John anymore because she doesn't have to feel overwhelmed with his problems—she can allow him to take care of them himself. Today, she's more comfortable with herself and with her children. She has changed both her attitude and her actions. It's not that she won't slip back—she has and she will— but she knows something different today, and so even when she does slip back, she knows the way out again.

Audrey has changed, too. First she had to do a lot of thinking about why her daughter's screaming affects her the way it does.

"It's like fingernails on a blackboard to me when she screams and cries. She can really cry, especially when she gets mad. That's the worst for me. I was brought up to believe that you shouldn't ever get mad, and I don't want her brought up that way. But somehow every time she does get mad, I have a reaction to it. I feel like it's always my fault, always something I should have done, one more thing and she wouldn't be this way. I keep asking her, 'What have I done to make you treat me this way? Why are you doing this to me?'

"She's ripping my skin open with her cries, and then she's tearing each nerve bloody. It's like she's torturing me. No, she *is* torturing me.

"And there's a certain cry of hers, one that gets to me even to think of it, a certain note of her cry, one that really destroys me. It sounds so familiar to me, so deep inside of me, it breaks me up. I can't move when she cries that cry, and it's a lucky thing because otherwise I might kill her. I want to kill that cry. For a long time I didn't know why that cry got to me. Then one day, in the midst of a crisis, I recognized it.

"That cry is *my* cry she's crying, I realized. That's *my* childhood cry. It's *my* misery, *my* pain, *my* cry from being beaten and sore and hurt. I hear myself crying somewhere deep inside of me when she cries my cry. It's me that's crying. And I can't let that cry go on one more second. Do you understand—that cry will kill me! It hurts so much, I'll die."

With help, Audrey is learning to cope with that cry. She is learning to separate her daughter's present cry from her own past cry, to remind herself that the two cries are not the same, that she and her daughter are two different people in two different times. To keep her mind focused, Audrey chants to herself, *That was then; this is now. That was then; this is now.* She marches around the house at the same time she chants, releasing tension both through her mind and through her body.

Everyone needs to discover his or her own way of coping with stress. Audrey chants. Sarah has a pillow that is meant especially for her to hit, to throw on the floor, and to scream at. She jumps on it, hits the floor and the furniture with it, punches it, and generally gives that pillow a tough time. Sometimes the pillow is her husband, at other times it's her children, and at still other times it's the world in general. That pillow takes all of the abuse she used to give to her family.

Hitting a pillow doesn't work for Judith, though. She told our PA group that she couldn't even think of doing something that would make her feel so silly. Judith agreed to try it, however, when she was told to stop worrying about how she would look when she was hitting the pillow and start thinking about how she looked when she was hitting her children. But the feeling of looking silly continued to outweigh the advantages of hitting the pillow, and she felt worse afterwards than she had to begin with. As she experimented in her mind with other people's suggestions, however, she thought that Charlie's favorite—kicking doors—might work very well for her. Apparently she didn't have the same inhibitions about the use of her feet and legs as she did about her arms and hands. She tried kicking, and she was right; she now kicks doors in every room of the house and feels hundreds of times better.

Doris' past conditioning makes her very uncomfortable with anything resembling anger or violence. Dancing relieves her tension. Doris dances out her anger in quick and jerky movements, in long and graceful ones. She puts her negative feelings into her movements and dances her pain away. She says that she can feel the stress rising to the surface, becoming perspiration on her skin, and then evaporating. As she finishes her dance, she is tired, thirsty, and free.

Our PA group had tried and tried to think of something Jennifer could do that would work for her. We suggested punching pillows, jumping up and down on the bed, running, washing walls, hammering meat, everything we could possibly think of. She had tried the things we had suggested, but none of them worked. The only thing that was even halfway effective was the telephone, but that wasn't always feasible because it took her almost forty minutes to begin to calm down. She didn't always have that kind of time. She needed to find something better and faster.

Then, one winter day, a station wagon got stuck in a snow drift in front of her house. Jennifer offered to help, and she marched straight up to that car. Within one minute it was free, and Jennifer was looking satisfied. "That felt good," she said.

Jennifer's release mechanism was going to be pushing cars! The amount of vital energy in her simply wasn't being used up by the physical activities that had been suggested. She's a big woman with a big life force, and she needed something big to release it and relieve her. Now she pushes her station wagon up and down the driveway and she feels much more in control. She has an alternative which fits her, one that comes closer to matching her own emotional strength.

Elaine buys china pieces at house sales. She buys the biggest and ugliest ones she can find. Her favorites are the figurines and the animals, but she'll use others if she has to. She has a special box for them. When things are hard for her, she takes one out and flings it against the wall. She throws it as hard as she can, and as she watches it shatter and the pieces fall down the wall, she feels much better.

Tracy jumps rope; Betty runs; and Carol writes. John hits counters, but he's trying to find something else now because he has broken their kitchen counter three times. Regardless of the physical outlet they use, though, everyone uses the telephone. This is always the first and the last option. As PA parents across the country say, "Reach for the phone instead of the kid."

In PA group meetings, participants look for new combinations of words and actions to relieve each person. One week it was Kay who wanted some help. Hitting a pillow is an old standby; Kay seemed to like that idea. Then we talked about the possibility of her screaming. Heather said that when she felt as if she would like to "bounce a kid off the wall" she went in between the storm door and the front door in her apartment, shut both doors tight, and screamed. "Who cares what the neighbors think?" Heather shrugged. "It's better than hitting the kids. They should be proud of me whenever they hear me yelling like that. It helps me and it's a lot better than what I'd be doing otherwise."

Heather has a very big voice and a very loud way of using it. We smiled as we pictured her closed into that little place yelling.

Admiringly, Kay looked at her and said, "That's so great. I mean, that's so great that you can do it."

"You could, too. There's nothing to it. You just let it fly," Heather assured her.

Kay laughed but looked frightened. "No, that's the one thing that really gets to me. When somebody yells or screams around me, that really sends me up the wall. That's the one thing I can't take. I can't handle that."

Heather had come from a home where screaming and yelling had been a tragic part of her childhood, so she picked up easily on what Kay was *not* saying. Heather moved a little closer to her.

"Kay, when you were little, was there much screaming in your house?"

"Yes, they used to yell at me before they...Well, yes, there was. So I could never scream. I think it's so great that you can, but I can't do that. Maybe I could throw pillows, but I could never scream." It was obvious that the idea of screaming tantalized her at the same time that it frightened her, though.

Kay left the meeting ready to throw pillows, to call someone for help if she needed it, and to think about screaming. She seemed to feel good as she left, as if she was better equipped for the life struggle. We all felt good.

Within days, our PA grapevine had it that Kay had screamed. At the next meeting the next week, we could hardly wait to hear her story, *our* story.

Kay began by saying that if we had designed the ultimate stressful sequence, we couldn't have done a better job. The telling was too much to organize, so she was just going to start from the beginning. As we all knew, their house was on the market to be sold. With five young children there was no way it could be in perfect order, and though it was always clean, toys and clothes had a way of appearing in strange places. She had been cleaning up the kitchen after serving lunch to nine children when the real estate man called to say that he wanted to bring people over in an hour.

Kay agreed and hung up the telephone. Then she looked at the house with more critical eyes and realized that there was much to be done. As she picked up the first dish to wash, Kay looked out through the kitchen window and saw one of the children fall off his bike. He came in crying, which woke up the baby, who also began crying. At that moment, another child came in with the news that the German shepherd had broken out of his kennel and was now trying to get into the rabbit cage. Then the oldest boy came in to say that his friend had just thrown the ball onto the roof and they couldn't play anymore, so would she please get the ball off the roof or could he get out the ladder and get the ball down himself? He thought that would be terrific. As she said no, another child came in and announced that the dog had made it into the rabbit cage and now had the pet rabbit in his mouth.

Kay went to the aid of the rabbit while the child who had fallen off his bike recovered, climbed back onto it, and cheerfully rode out into the street. She carried the not-quite-dead but certainly limp rabbit into the street with her as she retrieved the child on his bike and helplessly watched the dog go running off down the street. He never came when he was called, but Kay called a few times anyway—just in case—as she went back to the house.

She got the baby out of bed—where he was still crying—

and went to the telephone. It was Wednesday afternoon, not a good time to get a vet. She tried one after another, but they were all out. She stood there holding the telephone in one hand and dangling the rabbit in the other. The children came in with more good news: the neighbor said that Kay had better get her dog back or she was going to get reported. The rabbit died, and the child fell off his bike again. This time, he couldn't get up by himself, and he lay there crying while she ran out to help him.

He wanted to know why she was holding the dead rabbit, and the other boys wanted to know when she was going to get the ball off the roof. She got a ladder and climbed to the top of the roof.

While she was standing on top of the roof, Kay suddenly realized that if ever a time was perfect for a scream, this was it. So she drew in a huge chestful of air and put every last frustration into that scream. She let it fly, just like Heather had told her to. And out of her mouth came the tiniest, most pathetic squeak in the world. She said she almost turned around to see who'd made that silly sound. And all the kids crowded around the ladder.

"What happened, Mom? Are you okay? Where's the ball? What was that noise?

"Nothing. Yes. Here it is. Nothing," she sighed.

Resignedly, she climbed back down the ladder and went into the kitchen. She started to change the baby's diapers from his nap when she saw the rabbit and remembered that the real estate man was coming and the dog was still loose. She stood there quietly for a second, and then she saw the bees. If there's one thing in this world that Kay doesn't like, it's bees—and here were three of them circling her kitchen. They were the slow and sluggish kind, the kind that don't seem to be afraid of anything. One of the bees circled closer and closer to her. Her frantic attempts to wave him away only made her more available. He landed on her shoulder, and there he stayed. By this time she was so sweaty he was probably stuck there, but at any rate, he stayed. Meanwhile, the other two circled and circled overhead.

That was it; she called for help. She picked up the phone and dialed her husband. His boss answered, and as Kay began to blurt out something about rabbits and kids and roof, he tried to calm her down. When she got to the part about the "b-b-ees," he put Lloyd on the phone and then sent him home for a while.

Lloyd caught the dog and sent the neighborhood children

home and buried the rabbit while Kay changed the baby and cleaned the house and gave drinks to the children. They both took turns catching the child who alternately fell off his bike and rode it into the street. He wasn't very good at riding it yet.

As she finished her story, Kay said, "Now, why couldn't I have handled that by myself? Why did I have to call Lloyd?"

"Why, indeed?" we laughed. "Any Supermom would have been able to handle that before breakfast."

After we had finished laughing, we talked for a long time about how she not only *could* handle it, but in fact did handle it—that half of handling things is to know when to call for help. She had been right in every respect. She had tried to release her tensions by screaming. When that didn't work and she could no longer manage the situation, she had called for help. She had made it through an almost impossible situation, and she could even laugh about it. That was fantastic! And she had really screamed. Even if it hadn't been a very loud scream, it was her first, and she had done it. It was quite a change from her past responses to stress.

Parents who abuse can decide to change, and *they can and do change.* They can learn new ways to relate to their families. They can find alternatives to abuse. Parental resolve to change can be strong and beautiful; Todd has made his choice, and he'll stand by it.

"Okay, this is it. I don't care what it means; I don't care what happens; I don't care who knows. I know I can't go on this way. It's not worth it. I can't stand the look on her face, and how I feel. I can't live with the thought that I might kill her. How could I live with that? Every time I see a newspaper headline about child abuse, I wonder if I'll be the next one. Now I'm determined I won't be. I'm not going to take that chance. Things have got to get better for us. I don't care what it costs or how long it takes or what it means. I don't even care what they say to me or how they treat me. They can lock me up or take her away for a while if that's what we need. But I've got to change. I won't live like this anymore. Not one more day. I won't."

Chapter 10
The Implications of Change

A parent's choice not to abuse leads to a different pattern of behavior which influences the entire family. Change is hard and often threatening to friends and/or family members. One person's change demands corresponding or complementary changes of other persons close to him or her; this complicates the process.

Paul and Yvette are experiencing a change of major proportions. They have been married for eight years; their son, Keith, is six. Raised in families that were secretive and closed off from outside influences, neither Paul nor Yvette had ever learned to identify feelings—their own and others—or to separate feelings from actions. Quiet, withdrawn, first-generation, Italian Americans had raised Paul. They asked that their son be good, make money, get married, and follow the rules. Paul was ill-prepared for life with Yvette and Keith. It seemed incomprehensibly hectic for him. He defended himself against Yvette's explosive anger toward Keith by passively taking her side and quietly telling his son to listen to his mother. At other times, when Keith was spanked too hard or had his life threatened over the kinds of infractions that six year olds commonly commit, Paul watched the "disciplining" from a safe distance or busied himself with cleaning out his truck or doing some other household chores.

When Paul felt bad, he raided the refrigerator or slept late. He acted out his feelings in a passive and non-directed way. However, Paul's own survival demanded that he become minimally active, at least in the disputes which arose between Yvette and himself. Sometimes Yvette got angry over minor incidents, often literally spilled milk. Paul described his wife's appearance during one of these incidents: "Her whole body would stiffen up, her face would turn to stone, she would start saying how she was going to put me in a box [coffin]." Paul, somewhat frightened and not comprehending his wife's rage, would attempt to placate her. He would try to reason with her; he would ask her to "please settle down." Predictably enough, Yvette's anger would escalate to the point where she would start throwing dishes at Paul and tearing the house apart. At this extreme point, Paul, himself weighing two hundred and forty pounds, would tackle Yvette, who was half his size. He would then sit on her until all her anger and strength had been wrestled out. These bouts of acting out anger would be followed by days of mutual sulking, silence, and connubial separation.

Paul had learned to handle his angry feelings through basically passive measures while Yvette had learned to act hers out through both verbal and physical abuse. Yvette was physically abused as a child. She says, "If you didn't listen, you got a beating and that was that." As a child, she found herself being beaten for talking back, for spilling the milk, for stating her own age-appropriate opinions, and for making any remarks alluding to sex. All disagreements with her parents ended violently, for disagreements meant that you were "against" the other person. Being "against" the other person or having the other person "against" you was all too easy. If you didn't eat your dinner, you were against the other person. If you lost a sweater or some other garment, this was interpreted as being done against the parent. Yvette recounted one episode of disobeying a parental command given when she was ten years old.

"I was at my uncle's beach house with my parents and my brothers and sister. The mosquitoes were real bad and I'd been bitten right through my clothes. My whole body itched terribly. I couldn't stop scratching. When my parents couldn't stand my constant scratching any longer, they told me to completely undress so they could put some lotion on my body. I didn't want to undress in front of them, so I refused. At that point, I knew that something was going to happen. My mother has very fair skin—totally unlike mine. When I refused, her entire face began to get red from the neck up. You could see the blood moving up her face. As her face changed color, she threw me up against the wall and started beating me with her hands and fists. As I tried to get up, she threw me down and beat me some more. My father mostly watched, but he got in a few good licks. This continued until I couldn't get up any more. I was black and blue for a week. When my parents told you something and you didn't do it right away, you were asking for a beating."

Following a particularly bad abusive episode with Keith, after which the child had to stay home from school for two days, Yvette decided to seek help. When she told Paul that she wanted to go for help, he maintained that that was the wrong thing to do because Yvette didn't have a problem. She *did* sometimes overreact, he pointed out, but Keith was a difficult child—wasn't he? There was an obvious problem in their marriage—someone might get hurt someday—but what good would it do to talk about it to a stranger? After all, talking about it to each other hadn't helped.

Despite Paul's reluctance, Yvette did call for help. She told a PA worker that she was seeking help because she might seriously hurt her child, even kill him. As she came to trust the help offered to her, Yvette began to recite a depressing history of beatings. For a long time she had shut out her past; now the wounds needed to be reopened, examined, and remembered under a different light. Yvette began to understand that she was a "victim" and she became visibly angry over the kind of "deal" her parents had given her. Yvette began to see that she perceived and acted according to patterns learned from her parents. She learned that the men in her house—Paul and Keith—weren't always trying to "trip her up" and that if they sometimes made her angry or unhappy or simply didn't listen to her, this still didn't mean that they were "against" her.

"Well, how do I know they're not against me?" she asked.

"Well, I don't know what their intention is in every case, but one sure way would be to ask," she was told.

Generally, when Yvette was patient enough to ask and to wait for and listen to a reply, her explosive anger turned into a smile. She had to laugh at the irony between what she had imagined Paul and Keith meant and what they had really meant.

Yvette's relationship with Keith improved dramatically. His responses to her questions were quite literal and honest, and he loved to talk. He didn't need to run from her frozen expression any longer. During bad moments, when he did spill the milk once again, Keith "beat his mother to the punch" by asking her if she were angry at him. Through his own relentless inquiry, he modeled techniques of clarification for her. Prodded by his "parenting," Yvette became a much better mother. She read to him every night, meticulously followed his problems and progress in school, and finally, in her late twenties, learned to show real affection toward her child. She was able to touch him, hug him, care for him, and discipline him through a time out in his room when that response was most appropriate.

When Yvette started to become appropriately assertive and more open with her husband, Paul became frightened and withdrew. When she asked him if something were wrong, he said no and then stayed quiet the rest of the night. Paul gained weight and began to lose interest in his business. He also found himself increasingly alone at night with Keith. Yvette was out now most nights, feeling "born again" and proselytizing for PA. When she returned late at night, Paul—who had stayed up waiting for her—would argue about her lateness. He felt that this was simply "not right," but he wasn't able to recognize any feelings of anger or rejection on his own part.

By this time, the tables had been turned. Paul was losing *his* cool over spilled milk. At Yvette's suggestion, Paul came to PA for help and began to practice becoming more assertive. He explored the fantasized consequences of his assertive actions. These consequences were basically of two kinds—people wouldn't like him any longer or he would be beaten up. Paul was also able to see how his placating Yvette, by acting like a "namby-pamby," had triggered violent reactions in her. He was now prepared to take chances in expressing his own feelings.

When Paul began to assert himself and express his feelings, what he said often came out crudely, out of proportion, and even inaccurately. He had about ten years' worth of repressed feelings to handle. Moreover, Yvette hadn't had much practice in hearing Paul express feelings which weren't always positive toward her. He claimed that his problems had all started when he first met her, that if it weren't for her he would be happy, and that *she* was the problem, not he.

Even though she had been saying these same things to Paul for months, Yvette had difficulty accepting them. Paul felt euphoric with his newly found freedom, and Yvette felt hysterically angry. She wanted him to shut up, to go back to being quiet, to quit saying those hurtful things to her. She threatened him with all the old negative phrases that used to quiet him down, but they didn't work anymore. And so she used some new ones, but they didn't work either.

Even Yvette's pain isn't enough now to put Paul back into his shell, for he likes being a person with rights and feelings. She can't deny him that, but she just isn't certain she can live through this change with him. Paul doesn't want to hurt Yvette, but right now he is more important to himself than she is to him. He is going to be his own person, too, and Yvette wants that. She doesn't want to control him all the time—on some levels, she wants an equal—but the situation is hard for both of them as they learn to live through the changes involved in claiming their feelings. For the first time in Yvette's life, she is up against some opposition which she can't beat up. Nor will Paul satisfy her by beating her. Beat or be beaten have been the only two methods of coping with opposition that Yvette has ever known. Paul is up against a situation where he has so much to win that he can't bear to back away from the conflict. And so, for the first time in his life, he is standing up and fighting for his rights. It's hard for both of them as they design a new relationship. There's a lot of pain in their change. But that pain is tempered by the growing pleasure their steps toward wholeness give both of them and their son, Keith.

For Hank, the process of finding a new, different, and better way of responding to stress has been long and tedious.

"It doesn't seem fair. If I try to change myself, then I have to sell it to my wife and change her. She doesn't believe it's for the good, and she doesn't want me to change. She says I'm okay the way I am. Well, I'm not, but what she means is that she's scared, too. So we get used to the new me with a little change, and then I have to get the kids all used to that little change. And then when we are all comfortable with the new change, I go and change again in some different way, and it starts all over. No wonder it takes me so long; I'm not changing one person, I'm changing five people."

Allowing the family to readjust to each new configuration as family members change is a slow and complicated process. The children attempt to keep the parents responding in their familiar patterns, no matter how harmful those patterns might be. Children can and do provoke their parents to abuse them, almost as if to reassure themselves that their parents still care. After all, they have only known one kind of behavior from their parents, and they have accepted that behavior as the way their parents show love. Children are threatened by change and may provoke their parents to abusive actions to make sure they are the same people, the same old mom and dad that they knew a month ago. And it may be that they provoke them to prove to themselves that they, the children, can still control their parents.

For Evelyn, abusive episodes have a clearing effect, a purpose for her and for her son. She understands her feelings both before and after the abuse. What that means, however, is that she knows where to work, what feelings and actions need to be changed. It doesn't mean that she's able to avoid abusing her son now, though; the knowledge she has in her head is far different from the experiential knowledge she needs to avoid abusing. There is quite a gap between her intellectual and her emotional intelligence. It won't always be this way for her; she recognizes that this is just a time she is passing through.

"I'm not at all comfortable holding him. I don't like the

way he feels, I don't like to touch him at all, especially to change his pants. That really makes me kind of sick. I don't even like the way he looks down there. I guess I don't like much about him except when he's asleep. That's the only time I feel like I can relax. I'm always so uptight when he's awake. He looks at me as if he wants me to do something for him, and I don't know what to do. I don't like him looking at me, but he can't understand that. He always wants to be right near me, and I don't like that either. I can't get away from him.

"But all that changes when I finally explode. Then I want to be close to him, so close to him that I can really see him, so close to him that I can feel the breath of his crying on me. I like him to look at me then. When he won't, that just makes me madder. Everything's different when I'm hitting him.

"And it stays different afterwards. I'm relaxed and I don't mind holding him. I actually like it then. I even cuddle him a little. Not a lot, I'm still not too crazy about it; but after I hit him a lot, then I can hold him, too."

For Connie, too, the abuse changes her feelings.

"I feel different about him and about me, too, after I beat him. I think it starts out that I feel bad about me because of something I've said or done or not said or done. Then if he does anything that reminds me of myself, that's it. He's like me a lot, so of course he reminds me of me a lot. It's like I think I'm beating the ME out of HIM when I do it. Then afterwards I feel better about both of us. I take him to bed with me and we cry together and then we fall asleep together with me holding him in my arms and him holding me in his arms. It's kind of nice, if you know what I mean."

Both Diane's and Connie's children know what their mothers mean. The period after an abusive episode is warmer for them than any other time. When parents begin to work very hard to change their abusive behavior, children often perceive it as a threat. They fear the loss of those warm times they have learned to earn by suffering the abuse. It's a horrible truth that during the very times when parents are working the hardest to change their abusive patterns, their children are often working *their* hardest to provoke that same sorrowful behavior. This, of course, is part of the whole growing and changing process, but it is discouraging nevertheless. Change brings with it some amusing times as new responses are perfected. Recently Paula and Ralph, who both had come to PA for help, were sharing their son Bobby's bath time. This sharing was taking place not because they were feeling particularly good about each other and Bobby but because they were feeling tired. Ralph had been out of town all week, and Paula had had two cranky children in the house all that time. So now Paula was eager to have Ralph help parent the children. Ralph hadn't been doing this for very long, so they hadn't had much experience working together in this area.

As the end of the bath time approached, Bobby announced that he was not getting out of the tub. His parents insisted that he *was* getting out of the tub; he insisted again and still again that he wasn't. Soon the steamy bathroom was filled with the babble of angry and insistent voices. Ralph finally turned to Paula and yelled, "Okay, hit him. Now's the time to hit him."

"Why are you always telling *me* to hit him? Hit him yourself if you want him hit," Paula retorted. But that wasn't what she meant, and as she saw Ralph's face as he started towards Bobby, she said, "No, don't you remember that that's why we're going to PA—so we won't hit them when we're mad? Don't hit him," she ordered.

At that point, Bobby stopped screaming that he wasn't getting out of the tub and began to scream that they should hit him. "Hit me, hit me, hit me, hit me," he chanted. As Ralph reached for Bobby, Paula thrust herself between them, snatched Bobby out of the tub, pushed him into the hall, and threw a towel over him as he stood there. She then slammed and locked the bathroom door. Paula and Ralph huddled inside the bathroom; Bobby found himself outside. His scream turned into a startled clamor to be part of the group.

"What are you doing?" Ralph shrieked.

"I don't know, but I think it's better than hitting him, whatever it is," Paula responded shrilly.

"Well, now what?"

"I don't know. I guess he ought to get dressed." Paula went to the door and told Bobby that he should put his pajamas on, and that when he had them on, Mommy and Daddy would come out.

"Will he do it?" Ralph asked.

"I don't know," Paula replied. "Why don't we sit down?" And so they sat down, Ralph on the toilet and Paula on the edge of the tub as they waited and asked each other if Bobby was really going to put his pajamas on and if they were irrevocably hurting him by locking him out and themselves in. They waited as he quieted down, and they held their breaths as he went off to put on his pajamas. When Bobby did come back to tell them that he was ready, they knew for sure their spontaneous alternative was going to work. They unlocked the door, and then all three hugged each other.

Bobby said, "Next time I'll get out when it's time, and then you and Daddy won't get locked in the bathroom, right?"

"Right!" they agreed.

Section II
THE BEGINNINGS OF A SOLUTION

Chapter 11
Our PA Group Begins

The preceding chapters have dealt with individual people—who they are, how they got to be the way they are, and how they feel about themselves. But that's only half of the story of breaking the child abuse cycle. The other half has to do with how they are changing from parents who felt they were abusing their children into parents who are proud and fulfilled in their relationships with their children. This change, witnessed by all of us involved with a PA group, provides a hopeful message for everyone concerned with child abuse. The parents who seek the support of PA find healthy family-type relationships there. They learn what no one can learn alone—to trust and to problem-solve, to be dependent and to be independent, to experience and to avoid, to participate and to withdraw.

Obviously, no group initially comes together as a close and sharing family. At first they must hazard the risk of trusting their lives to strangers. In fact, each person brings with himself or herself fears, insecurities, and defenses built up over a lifetime. Even the willingness to tackle and solve problems, to try something new, is somewhat crippled because past experience hasn't brought them much success in these areas.

Our PA chapter began after several people from the same area called in to our central number. Together, we arranged to meet at a neighboring church where separate rooms would be available for us and for the children. We found a person to care for the children while we held our meetings. Our first meeting was planned for one Friday afternoon in the late winter.

The morning of that first meeting I called Vicki only to discover that we already had our first problem. I had planned to drive her and her two children to the meeting, and I was checking to make sure we were all set. At first her voice sounded flat over the telephone. "What happened to you last week? Where were you?" she asked.

Her question startled me. "Last week? I was still out of town last week. You waited for me last week?" I had that sinking sensation that she had, even as I asked the question.

"Yes, I did." Vicki sounded despondent. She had been let down again.

What could I say except, "I'm sorry; there's been a misunderstanding; but I'll be there today for sure. I'll see you in just a few minutes, and we'll go to the meeting."

But Vicki was adamant. "No, not this week. Don't come this week. I can't make it this week. It was really bad last week. I waited outside with the kids for you for an hour last week. I hadn't slept very well the night before, so I was already in bad shape. Then when you didn't come, I had one of those wars with the boys that I was going to come to PA to *stop* having. Last week is too fresh in my mind. I can't come this week. Maybe next week."

I asked Vicki to reconsider, to change her mind, to please come, but she refused. She insisted that she wouldn't come this week. Finally, I said I'd come to her house anyway. If she were ready, we'd go together. If not, at least I would know where she lived and what she looked like for next week.

To my joy and relief, Vicki had decided to come by the time I arrived at her home. With her two boys, Lenny and David, we went to the meeting. We met in the church kitchen. Ruth and Mary were already there when we arrived, and Wendy came soon after that with her children, Kim and Sherry. When Anna and Jody came with their children, the seven of us who had agreed to meet were together for the first time. In future weeks men and other women joined us, but for our first meeting we seven were the group.

We were nervous at that meeting. The group was new, and the subject was heavy. "Child abuse" is a strong label, and each person there identified herself as a person who at least feared the possibility of being a child abuser. Each person there was meeting other people who also feared child abuse, and although each person knew what she herself looked like, no one could visualize a roomful of child abusers, a roomful of people who acted out the unspeakable, who hurt or might hurt their own children. To everyone's surprise the group looked very much like any other group of attractive young mothers.

One thing that was different in this group, however, was the amount of commitment each person was bringing to the group itself. Each woman in the room was there because of love for her children and a desire to make things better for her family. Each person was willing to do whatever was necessary to change a situation she had found intolerable. The beginning of this change included coming to a meeting to prevent child abuse with a number of strangers one was committed to trying to trust.

The fact that no one knew anyone else made sharing easier in the beginning. Since no one knew what role she was expected to play, it was easier to be honest and natural. There were no standards to measure up to and no need to play games.

106

This room, in which seven women nervously sat, provided a safe place to talk about child abuse.

To begin our first meeting, each woman gave her first name and shared a little of why she had come. Mary, as chairperson, began. "My name is Mary and I'm here because I'm very afraid of what might happen with my kids, of what I feel like doing to them. I can't always stay on top of things, and when I can't, I take it out on the kids. I don't want to do that anymore."

As sponsor, I went next. "My name is Chris, and I believe that both parents and children are entitled to a good experience together. That doesn't always happen naturally. But I believe that with groups of people working together good things can happen, and I'd like to help that happen."

During her turn to share, Vicki admitted, "I smack my kids around a little too much. No, let's be honest and cut the B.S. I smack my kids around a *lot* too much, and I want to stop it."

Wendy was next. "I don't exactly have trouble with just my kids; it's more my temper in general. Last week I ripped out a banister. I think I need help."

Jody's voice was soft and quiet. She confided, "I don't want to do to my kids what my parents did to me. But I don't know how to do anything else. I want to learn to do better. I don't know how."

Ruth, with her quick words and her choppy hand motions, darted in next. "Well, I don't have an abuse problem. It's my daughter, though. She's been so bad since the new baby came. I scream at her constantly, and I can't stand the sight of her. What should I do? It's not abuse, I just need some answers?"

Anna covered her face with her hands and cried as she told us why she had come. "I'm here because I hurt my son, I hurt him badly and I don't ever want that to happen again."

In the next few months we welcomed Kandy, who told the group, "I scare myself. I scream at them so much. I hate it. I can't control myself."

And Fran: "After an episode with them, I'm so hoarse I can't even talk. I can only whisper, and I know I've hit them again for no reason at all. What if the neighbors hear? I'm so ashamed of the way I am."

Rosemary had a hard time getting to meetings. But her voice revealed how severe her need was. "I'm sick so much of the time, I mean physically sick. I've had so many things wrong with me that no one even believes me anymore. I don't even remember Tommy much as a baby, and now I need some help—I need a lot of help."

Jean came with only the explanation, "My pediatrician said I should come." But that reason was enough for the group. We welcomed anyone who wanted to talk about child abuse.

Kathy came into the group quietly and determinedly. "My daughter's not growing right. But when I took her into the doctor, he said that it's me who has the problem—it's me making her not grow. That's not right, so I'm here to get help."

Kathy's sister, Carole, also came. She laughed and said, "Kathy is always yapping about PA, and I want Marty to have a good childhood. So here I am."

Bee blew in with a flurry. "I told my husband that if we ever had a baby, he'd have to help. Well, he's helping. In fact, he's doing most of it. I'm blowing it. I abuse my child, and I want help."

Beverly crept in with "Well...I don't really know....I just don't think I'm a very good mother....I don't even feed them....I'm a terrible mother...."

With the assurance that we were establishing a safe place to talk about mutual problems and to change relationships at home, we began to establish our own identity as a group. Early in our history, we gave ourselves a name. Vicki was putting the soft drinks into the refrigerator one day when she found a treasure—a vase full of tulips. She set the vase in the middle of the table and said, "This is it, folks—last week fresh azaleas and this week fresh tulips. What next?"

As she was talking, we all looked at the vase. It was filled with lovely yellow variegated tulips and one purple one. The purple tulip stuck out to one side, and as Vicki talked, she rearranged the flowers until the purple one nestled down in the middle of the yellow ones. "There, that's better," she said, stepping back to admire her handiwork.

Someone observed that there must be a message we could learn from those flowers, so we began to think of all the ideas they might be illustrating: "Flowers are everywhere, even in the refrigerator....Things look better in the light....Crime pays.... Tulips don't have leaves....Cold water makes us shut up.... Everything looks better in the center of things."

Then someone happily found the message we had all been looking for—"Every one of us feels like the purple tulip in a vase full of yellow tulips." And so that message, that feeling, became our name: The Purple Tulips.

We used those tulips until they fell apart and were nothing but stems. Then someone brought in plastic tulips, some yellow and some purple. Now they make up half of our centerpiece at each meeting. The other half is our facial tissue box painted by one of our members with symbols of the group on it: the purple tulip, of course; a butterfly and a caterpillar to represent the possibility of change in our lives; a jagged line of anger; dark colors of depression; and beautiful colors of hope, beauty, and love. The tissue paper box gets a lot of use. Symbolically, the paper box states that it's okay to cry. Practically, the box of facial tissues is very convenient. Tears of both joy and sorrow are frequent in our meetings.

We began each meeting with an open-ended statement which we took turns completing. We learned about ourselves and about each other through these beginnings. Some weeks we were very subject-oriented with openers like "I feel guilty when I..." or "The thing that my child does that drives me the craziest is ...." Sometimes we were introspective with statements such as "When I was little, I was afraid of ... I have trouble with that fear today in this way..." or "The reason it's hard for me to be honest is because ...." We were accomplishment-oriented some weeks with "One thing I did last week that I'm proud of is ..." or "One thing I did last week that I'm not so proud of is ...." We dreamed and set goals with openers like "If I could be anything in the world, I would be ..." and "I wish I were ...."

We got to know each other by describing ourselves. Each member would say, "Three things you would have to know about me to really know who I am are that I ... and ... and ...." We gave each other feedback by saying "One thing I really like about you is ...," and we gave thanks by saying "One thing I'm grateful for this week is ...."

Our first meetings were characterized by specific questions and answers, problems and suggestions. People had come because they were having trouble dealing with their children. One of the first things they needed was a variety of new ways to relate to their children. We readily shared answers and techniques and insights we had each discovered on our own. The problems the members faced were not as unique as they had feared, and the sharing of solutions was specifically helpful.

From the beginning, the group members tried to talk about problems in a helpful and nonjudgmental way. Gradually we grew to trust each other's responses and intents. There was the usual need for clarification, but in general, the atmosphere was supportive and freeing.

The first problems brought to the group were tangible ones which had an immediacy to them. Ruth was concerned about her daughter, Gail. "When Gail plays with other kids, she acts like a selfish bully. She won't share. It's really embarrassing for me in front of my friends. She hangs on to her toys like I never give her any, and she won't share."

Ruth was impatient with Gail and feared that the stress of this impatience might lead to abuse. Obviously, Gail didn't know how three year olds usually act and was distressed at her daughter's seeming selfishness.

Vicki's son was about the same age as Gail's daughter, so Vicki offered one possible solution. "Do you *make* her share everything? Maybe you should give her a few things that she doesn't have to share. Let her choose a few things that are just hers. Then maybe she won't mind sharing the rest."

Mary gently but sadly reminisced about her own childhood. "When I was little, my parents used to make me share everything. I grew up thinking that they cared more about every other person in the world than they did about me."

Anna's children were a little older. "She's only three, isn't she? My kids didn't understand anything about sharing at all until a little later than that."

Kandy and Kathy had both been working on getting their children to share. Kandy offered, "I make Sarah play alone if she doesn't feel like sharing. She doesn't have to share, but if she's going to play with other children, then she does have to share. She always has her choice though."

The group wondered if something else besides her distress over Gail's not sharing might be going on inside Ruth. "Are you totally concerned about *her* sharing? How does it make you feel to have her make you look like a bad mother in front of your friends, like a mother who can't even teach her child to share?"

"Yeah," Ruth admitted. "There sure is some of that, too. I can handle her not sharing at home, I don't really care. There are plenty of toys around, but when my friends are around, I want her to make me look good. It's harder with other people watching." Ruth thought about this for a while. Then she thanked the group for their help and said, "You've given me a lot to think about for next time. I'll let you know how it goes."

As the weeks passed we discussed many problems—child abuse, guilt, sexuality, suicide wishes or attempts, mothers-in-law, friends, husbands, and marriages. The experience of being with people who could understand and accept became almost euphoric for the members. One day Anna verbalized the feelings of the whole group when she said, "Just to know I'm not the only one in the world who feels this way means so much to me!"

Between meetings, telephones rang constantly. Members gave one another daily support. Bags of clothing, food, curtains, and almost everything else imaginable passed back and forth at a dizzying pace. We helped each other out with words and the sharing of experiences, with loving concern and the sharing of tangible signs of our care. Whenever a new baby arrived, some member who had a toddler shared the baby clothes she'd put to use months before. When the children arrived at each weekly meeting, their clothing always excited comment. "Oh, I remember that dress. It looks so cute on Sarah." Or, "That's the suit he wore for my third cousin's wedding, and he cried the whole time."

There were other signs of caring going on, too. At the time when we first began meeting together, Vicki hadn't been divorced for very long, and she was only just learning how to live with her children and no husband. She had what she termed frequent "attacks of the lonelies." The group members didn't know what to say to her, how to ease her loneliness, or how to help her. During one of Vicki's "attacks," Anna decided that she had had enough of that futile feeling of not doing anything. She got in her car, drove over and picked up Vicki and her two sons, Lenny and David, and took them all home with her for the weekend. They did that several times during the next few months, and Vicki and her children had the opportunity to be in a family, to have company, and to avoid the "lonelies." Anna had the chance to have the company of a friend and to help Vicki. Learning to spend long periods of time with other people is, of necessity, a growing experience. Vicki and Anna both discovered new ways of relating to each other and to their children; they found out new things about themselves and about each other; and they got to know each other better. They learned to ask for help, to be specific about what they needed. When one of them was feeling a little uptight, the other would watch the children while the uptight one did dishes or laundry or some other manual task-oriented work. They learned that half of being independent is being dependent, and they learned to cope by knowing when to ask for help.

Too often, when people are having trouble as a family, our first solution is to split up the family. This can be counter-productive. While some families do need to be separated, others do not. Instead, they need to learn how to live together. They need to be cared for as a whole family unit, not as a group of unrelated individuals. By separating them so quickly, we lose the chance to help them work out their relationships together.

The opportunity to observe other families living together is valuable and beneficial. Having seen Vicki's family in operation, Kandy confided to the group one day, "I didn't know how to set limits for my kids. If I ever tried, I couldn't make them stick. But Vicki is good at that. She tells her kids what she expects from them, when she expects it, and what will happen to them if they don't do it. She means it, and her kids mind. Now it's a little easier for me because I at least know the words to say and how to say them. It's easier for my kids, too. They've seen that her kids have to mind, and so they know they're going to have to do the same thing. They know what's expected of them, too."

Vicki, in turn, had learned something from observing Kandy and her children. "I never even thought of listening to my kids before, but Kandy does. When her kids say they don't want to do something, she asks them why. I never thought of asking my kids why. I never even thought that they might have a reason. They just did what I said—*period, or else.* But I like to see the way Kandy treats her kids, like they were people. I'm going to try that with my kids, too."

As the weeks passed, the focus of our meetings changed from the search for answers to the awareness of the process. We no longer spent so much time on specific answers, though those were often needed and given. We spent more time on personality issues because parenting takes place effectively and positively from an effective and positive person. We discovered that when people feel good about themselves, they also feel good about their children. And when they don't feel good about themselves, they can't feel good about their children.

Kandy wailed the question one week, "How can I give what I don't have? How can I fill other people's needs when no one is filling mine?"

Jean couldn't even cope with that question yet. "At least you know you aren't getting your needs met. I don't even know what my needs are!"

Vicki knew, but that wasn't enough. "What difference does it make anyway? There's no one around for me."

Ruth wasn't ready to admit defeat or get trapped in any emotional quicksand that easily. She retorted, "Well, then what else can you do? There must be a way. Let's figure it out." Ruth was always ready to solve a problem, to look at things a new way, to find an answer.

In the past, Vicki had quietly sat by while Ruth "solved" her problems for her. Afterwards, however, Vicki felt mad, resentful, angry, and guilty. This time, as Ruth began the expected ritual, Vicki changed the pattern by angrily saying, "Well, one thing I do need is a place where I can feel sorry for myself if I want to; a place where I can cry because I'm sad." Vicki didn't want Ruth to "solve" her problem that easily, and she made that clear.

Ruth understood and slowly replied, "Okay, I hear you. I have an awfully hard time not making everything all better, and it really frustrates me when I can't. But I'll try to stop mothering you and the whole world, too!" The group just looked at her. The silence became heavy and she continued, "Well, did you think I didn't know? I knew. I just didn't know what else to do. Do you have any idea of how hard it is for me *not* to have the answer? I wasn't ready to risk it yet. Now I am, that's all." What could we do? We grinned at each other and at Ruth.

Jody had been looking interested during this part of the conversation, but for most of the time before it, she had been looking very uncomfortable. Now she shared her feelings. "But what do the *children* need? That's the question. We spend too much time talking about ourselves and not enough time talking about the children."

Apparently Anna had been thinking about this, too, because her response was firm, energetic, and thoughtful. "For me, Jody, I can really say that the only times I hurt the children are when I don't take care of myself. When I'm upset or angry or sad or in any way needy and I don't do something about it, that's when I hurt them. When I don't take care of me, I can't take care of them. When I do take care of me, then I can take care of them." Anna paused and then continued, "The only problem is

113

that I don't always know how to take care of myself."

Our PA group worked together beautifully during those first few weeks. But as every honeymoon ends, so did ours. Each person in the group began to wonder if perhaps she was in the wrong place after all. Although we had been meeting together for quite a while, there were still problems. Things were better for each member, but they weren't perfect yet. So each person in turn decided that she wasn't right for the group—her problems were either too severe or not severe enough. Each person decided that she was either pushing the group ahead too fast or holding the group back. She was too quiet or too loud, too time-consuming with her problem or too unwilling to share, too weak or too strong. Although each reason sounded different, the feeling behind each reason was the same. Each person was thinking, *I don't belong anywhere, and here is no exception. They say they like me, but that's because they don't know all about me and how bad I really am. I'd better drop out before they find out more about me because they wouldn't like me if they knew the real me, and it's too good to be true this way.*

Anna said that since her loss of control with her son led to physical abuse, her problems were worse than anyone else's. Therefore, she'd better drop out.

Ruth felt that since her own nonphysical loss of control with her daughter didn't leave any visible wounds, her problems weren't as bad as anyone else's. Therefore, she'd better drop out.

Anna stayed home from the next meeting, but Ruth missed her. She called her after the meeting and said, "Anna, where were you? I really missed you. It's not the same without you. Please don't miss any more!"

Then Ruth didn't come one time. "Where's Ruth?" Anna asked. "How is she? Has anyone talked to her? How are her kids? Is she okay? What's going on with her?"

It turned out that it didn't matter who had the worse or the better problem. Both Anna and Ruth liked each other, and they cared enough to talk about it. Neither of them mentioned dropping out after that.

Wendy was too embarrassed even to say that she felt she was holding the group back, so she just decided to stop coming. She thought that by staying away she wouldn't have to face any of us or any of her own problems. We were beginning to get very close to some very basic problems for her.

But the afternoon that Wendy failed to come to the

meeting, someone thought that Wendy might be feeling the way she was, and so the group got into a car and drove over to her house. Wendy's eyes were red from crying when we got there. Every woman who crowded into her living room was overwhelmed that someone could care enough about our group, about us, to cry when she missed a meeting. Each person had thought she was the only one who cared that much about the meetings. And the tangible evidence of caring for Wendy made every person feel cared for and valuable because she was a member of this group, too. Wendy said that she darned well wasn't about to have every meeting at *her* house, and if that was her only alternative. . . . Everyone smiled at that. "Yes," we said, "That's the only alternative." Wendy laughed, put her hands on her hips, and assumed a disgruntled pose. "Well," she said, "in that case I won't miss another meeting."

And then Mary helped the group to face the realization that Wendy's not coming to the meeting combined with our response forced on us. "We all still feel as if we're the only purple tulip. No matter how close we get to each other, that feeling's still there. So let's just be aware and, when we feel it, just remind ourselves that everyone feels it sometimes, too."

We were closer to having a good family relationship by that time. At the beginning of our group life, we had been afraid things were too good to be true. And we were right—they were. People aren't always as nice and giving and kind and receptive as we had been with each other at first. Sometimes we got bitchy, demanding, selfish, and greedy. We let each other down, and we got let down. We asked too much, and we didn't give enough. We were petty and uncaring.

But luckily we took turns. When one of us was nasty, another was nice. When one was petty, another was inspired. We didn't all get selfish and greedy at the same time. We survived our own realities and found ourselves flexible enough to accept the failings of each other as well as our own. We didn't always feel wonderful about each other, but we did feel good about the group and committed to it and to each other. That's the sign of a good group.

There were some things that could be done to discover and then meet people's needs, but there were also some problems that remained out of our reach. We tried to determine ownership of problems, to discover which ones we could legitimately worry about and which ones actually belonged to someone else. It was a difficult concept for the members to grasp. Most of the PA parents had very little experience of their own power in a healthy way; they were just starting to realize their own ability to change, influence, or control a situation. They had had no practice in learning to differentiate between those problems which they might reasonably be able to affect and those over which they had no power. They were accustomed to thinking of any problem anywhere near them as their own personal problem, their own fault, and their own responsibility. It was Vicki who one day finally put the concept we were struggling with into clearly understandable words and images. Jody had told her that she had wanted to ask something but that she didn't want to make Vicki uncomfortable or hurt her feelings.

"Listen, Jody," Vicki said. "You ask me anything you want. My feelings are my bag of shit, and I'll play in my bag when I want to. You keep your hands in your own bag of shit and ask me anything you want." From then on, we rejoiced to have such a simple question to clarify ownership of problems— "Whose bag of shit is it?"

Chapter 12
Learning to Accept Ourselves

Membership in a PA group brings fast and strong changes for its members. That's what they want; that's why they called; that's what they're after. They and their families were in trouble, and they called for help. With all the love and energy they invest in making life better for their families and themselves, along with PA's support and techniques, it's no wonder positive change occurs rapidly.

However, change brings its own set of problems and difficulties. When each person first called for help, she or he had a sense of personal identity, albeit a negative one. After spending time with other parents, receiving help and then giving help, each person sees that he or she isn't so isolated, so bad, so weird, or so alone. As time in a PA support group passes, members admit that perhaps some parts of their personality might be actually attractive, helpful, and positive; they also realize that those parts of themselves that are negative don't have to stay that way. They learn that they can change and can continue to unfold into increasingly more positive people *if they choose.*

For a while the realization that they can become more whole individuals leaves PA members without much sense of identity. Anna first verbalized this loss of identity. "I know I'm not the same person that I was, but now I don't have any idea who I am. It scares me sometimes. Who the heck am I?" We tried to say that her not being able to explain who she was didn't matter. Just because she couldn't put herself into neat little word packages didn't mean she didn't exist. Moreover, any neat little word packages she did come up with would be obsolete almost immediately, because Anna was always changing. If she stopped to classify herself, she'd miss herself; by the time she'd decide which box to put herself into, she'd no longer fit there. Who she was couldn't be answered that simply. Who she was was a person *becoming.* Our answer didn't solve Anna's problem of *wanting* to be able to put her identity into words, however.

Anna's problem was easy for Kandy to identify with. She'd been having serious back trouble for a long time and finally had made an appointment to see the doctor. She admitted, "The reason I didn't go to him for so long was because I was afraid he'd send me to the hospital or to bed. I thought I could tough it out, and I did just that for a long time. I can't stand the idea of having to stay in bed. How can I even think of it with the kids? I have to take care of them, and I have to take care of the house. I have to do it."

"Why? Why do you *have* to do it?" we asked.

Kandy took a deep breath and began, "I'll try to condense all of what I've been thinking these weeks....If I can take care of the house, Bob, and the kids, then I know who I am. I'm a housekeeper, a wife, and a mother. That's who I am. But if I can't do it all, if I can't clean the house and can't take care of the kids and can't take care of Bob, then what am I? I'm a failure or a nothing. I don't want to be either of those things."

"You must feel terrific when you go to the bathroom, don't you?" someone responded.

"Huh?"

"Well, if you're a failure when your back fails, then you must be a success when your bladder succeeds, right?"

"No, that's different. I don't control that. Oh, I see what you're saying. Yes, that's right. I guess I do feel responsible for my back, and I do feel like I've failed because I can't be up and functioning. I think I ought to be able to do it. I know in my head I shouldn't feel that way, but I can't help it."

"Kandy, suppose, just suppose, that you had to go to bed and lie there for the rest of your life. Suppose the worst — suppose that you'd be in bed for your whole life. Does that mean you'd cease to exist? Does that mean you'd be a nobody? Does that mean you'd never laugh or smile again? Does it mean the end of your life, of your being? Suppose you never ever cleaned house again, would that mean you weren't a mother? Suppose you couldn't make meals or wash clothes — wouldn't you still be there? Wouldn't there still be a heap of Kandy in the bed and wouldn't that heap be you? You'd still be you, wouldn't you? You'd still be lying in bed, and you'd still be you. You wouldn't disappear, and you wouldn't turn into nothing. You'd still be you! Just because what you did disappeared, *you* wouldn't!"

Wendy said, "I think I might know something of what you're feeling, Kandy. You know how I'm feeling about Hank right now. You know I'm thinking I might be better off without him. I might be a better mother, a better person, a better everything, and maybe a lot happier. But I'm not sure. I don't know. Can I really do it without him? Do I really even want to? I don't know. I know I could manage the kids; I've done that when he's been overseas. He's probably going again, but even when he's gone, I'm still being his wife. I don't know if I can be just me. I don't know if I can handle it if I'm not a wife. At least I

118

know who I am when I'm married."

"Yes, that's it," Kandy nodded her head as she agreed.

Mary understood, too. "I remember when Rick, my therapist, said he didn't like me. Well, that's not exactly what he said, but he did say we couldn't be friends the way I wanted to be friends, and I heard it that he said he didn't like me. It didn't take much for me to play the rest of it out in my head all by myself. He doesn't like me; therefore, I'm not worth liking, and nobody will like me. If people don't like me, I'm no good, and if I'm no good, I might as well go ahead and kill myself."

"Mary, is Rick always right, absolutely every time, always right?"

"Well, no one is *always* right."

"So then, even if he *did* say he didn't like you (which he didn't say), even if he did say it, that wouldn't mean you weren't likeable. It would just mean *he* didn't like you. If we like you, and we do, does that mean everyone will like you and that you're likeable? No, it only means we like you. Actually Rick likes you, too, and you know it. But you're who you are no matter who likes you or doesn't like you. You're you."

Ruth had yet another angle on the same subject. "I feel like I'm not me—a nonperson, a failure—when my kids misbehave. I can take it if someone doesn't like me; I don't expect everyone to like me. But I do expect my kids to be good all the time. I expect them to be perfect angels all the time, and when they aren't, that's when I have trouble. I'm sure that if they misbehave, it's because I didn't mother them right. And if I'm not a good mother, then I'm a rotten person, a thoroughly rotten person. I feel as if I'm responsible for every bad thing they do—not every good thing, just every bad thing. I only feel good when they're being wonderful, and then come to think of it, I'm always nervous about when they're going to start being bad. No wonder I'm always so tired!"

Independent identity is neither easy to find nor to keep. To know and to accept the reality of existence outside of performance, outside of roles and functions, outside of other people's expectations, is challenging. Kandy thought she'd found her identity in her ability to perform her tasks, to fulfill her functional responsibilities. When she was facing the possibility of being unable to live her role for a while, she felt threatened. Wendy had found her sense of identity as Hank's wife, and the thought of living without that label made her fearful. For Mary, her identity had often been found in other people's perceptions of her, and when her therapist seemed less than totally affirming of her, she questioned her entire worth as a person. Ruth's identity lay in a job well-done; her well-behaved children reflected her own worth. She couldn't see herself as being separate from her children's behavior.

To claim value as a person and then to translate that claim into action was even harder for PA members than finding an identity. Jody told us about her struggle. "I'm not used to thinking I'm a person, that I count. It's not easy for me to believe that I have rights. And when I do finally stick up for my rights, I feel so darned guilty afterwards.

"Last week, for instance, I'll tell you what happened. I have a special bucket I use for cleaning. I know I've talked about it before; Phil and I fight about it all the time. It's a big deal to me. It's probably silly, but it doesn't seem silly to me. I use it for almost all my cleaning. It fits on the stairs, and I use it for floors and for walls, for everything. It's mine. But Phil keeps taking it out to the garage. Whenever he wants a bucket, he just helps himself to mine, and he puts his brushes in it, or he washes his car or anything he wants. And then he leaves it out there for me to go get and for me to wash and for me to bring back in.

"I've told him hundreds of times, 'Clean it and bring it back or don't use it.' But he doesn't do either. He just leaves it out in the garage filthy and dirty. It makes me mad, really mad. And I don't like to get mad; it scares me when I get mad. I don't like it at all.

"So, anyway, last week he took the bucket, got it all dirty again, and left it there in the garage. Well, this time so did I. I just left it right there, too. I wasn't going to touch it, and I didn't. So, consequently, I did any of the jobs around the house that I needed the bucket for.

"It took a while, but finally one day Phil looked at the floor and then at me. He said, 'The floor's dirty, Jody.'

"I just went on wiping the counters, and I was just as polite to him. 'So's the bucket, Phil,' I said. He didn't say anything at all. He just went out and got the bucket and brought it in all clean and dry. Now tell me, all of you, why do *I* feel guilty?"

"Don't worry," Ruth assured her. "Just hang in there. In no time at all, you'll scarcely notice a twinge of guilt. You may have to force yourself at the beginning, but keep it up. Insist;

demand. You *are* a person. Keep it up, you'll love it. Phil might not, but you will."

We returned to the theme of identity and value again and again in our meetings and daily telephone calls, because learning to feel good about one's identity is hard. So, first we learned to take pleasure in the identity of our group; we learned to accept the personality of our group; and we learned to talk about what our group might be needing. To talk of the inadequacies and weaknesses of something we were all a part of—the group—was easier than talking about them in one another. And to talk of times when the group didn't meet our needs was easier than talking of times when we didn't meet one another's needs.

For many PA parents, honest communication is a difficult skill to acquire. For their past has been filled with arguments and silences, tears and denials. Rational and open disagreement has been an impossibility. They have had no place to learn the skill of differing, either in perceptions, opinions, or feelings. And so we tried to learn to give each other feedback about the group. We managed that step fairly smoothly, and then we went on to try to give each other feedback about one another.

For a few weeks, this proved to be a disaster. One person told another that what the latter had said three weeks ago had hurt her feelings, so we talked about the need for promptness in feedback. Another person in the group told someone else that she didn't like the way she related to her, so we talked about the need for specific tangible suggestions. A third group member told how she had been unable to sleep all night because of something someone else had said, and we talked about the difference between feedback and blaming. And when another person expressed her discomfort about someone to everyone other than the person she was uncomfortable with, we discussed the difference between gossiping and feedback. All in all, this was a tearful and traumatic time as we learned to handle our new skill, but eventually we got better at it. It was a good thing, too, because we needed it soon after.

As a group concentrating on our good points, we neglected to acknowledge our limitations. One day we harvested the crop of our unreal expectations. As Mary, our chairperson, walked into the meeting, she didn't look very well. She was pale, her eyes were dark and swollen, and her posture was strained. I watched her as the meeting progressed. She was responding well to people—thoughtfully, caringly—but perhaps a trifle too quickly. She was trying not to let IT show, whatever IT was. I tried to think about what IT might be; what she might need; what we could do; what might be lacking for her. But I was at a loss.

She was in PA, and she seemed to be getting a lot out of the meetings. We were all taking a Yoga class at a separate meeting once a week, and she was having individual therapy twice a week. I knew that each session was running well over an hour. She was also receiving relaxation therapy twice a week. She was using the taped recordings of the technique with some of the other members who wanted it now, too. She had been elected to the PA Board, which was a concrete statement of her ability. She did public speaking occasionally and was developing a natural ease in her radio, TV, and personal appearances. She knew she did a good job, and she reached many people. She was doing an excellent job as a chairperson; members were calling her for help, and her responses and presence were enabling much growth. She had to feel good about that. She seemed to be doing well with her husband and her children. What could be lacking? Why did she look the way she did?

And then the answer hit me as I saw her stifle a yawn. She was exhausted! That was all there was to it; and as I thought again about all she was doing, this made sense. She was having to be superhuman just to appear where she had to appear when she had to be there. So I said, "Mary, you're doing so much right now. How are you doing it all?"

"Oh, it's okay. I'm getting it done. I'm fine, everything's just fine," she said as she looked at the floor.

"Do you like it? Are you having a good time? How's your family handling it?"

"Well..." She looked up almost desperately, and then she overflowed. "My family's not doing very well at all, and neither am I. I walk in from being away so tired I can hardly stand it, and then the kids are all over me. They're so wild, I can't take it. But I know they've missed me, and I want to be with them. They come first in my life, but I don't seem to live that way. My husband thinks I care more for everyone else than I do for him. He says I never have time for him. He knows it's not true, but he feels like it is. He says he's thinking of going down the street and calling me on the phone so I'll talk to him. And every time we try to talk, the phone rings and it's someone needing me. But what can I do? How can I say no when someone needs me? I don't

122

know what I'm going to do."

"Why didn't you tell us?" The group was surprised and ashamed.

"It's not your fault. I didn't tell you because I didn't want to let you down."

We talked for a while about that, and then she went on. She was still quiet, but not as quiet. "And there's maybe even more to it than that. I guess maybe I was afraid that if I let you down, you wouldn't like me anymore. You'd be sorry you'd called, and you're my friends, and I don't want to lose that. You all mean too much to me."

We talked about how hard it is to set limits for ourselves as individuals and as a group, and how hard it is to stick to our enforced limits. It's difficult to accept limitations, to acknowledge them openly, and to remember they exist. Setting limits also means that we run the risk of finding out whether people like us for ourselves or for what we're doing for them. That's risky, the group admitted; risky for anyone, but especially risky for people who are only just beginning to think there might be something worth liking in themselves.

Mary had demonstrated and verbalized the problem, but each person identified with her. Everyone in our group had trouble setting realistic limits and then staying within them without feeling guilty, martyred, or inadequate. But the whole point of being involved in this group was to make life better for families, and if the involvement began to make life worse, then the point was lost. We laughed as one of us said, "If people aren't going to like us when they find out how human we were, then we might as well find this out in the beginning to save us all a lot of time and trouble!"

The group gratefully went back to being honest and comfortable again, discussing even how things were *not* the way they should be. No one had to cope well every day and do better and better each week. We wanted to admit that we were only human and that we never had been and never would be perfect. As Jean put it, "I'm not okay, and you're not okay—but that's okay."

One of our next meetings took place on a definitely "not okay" day. The weather was rainy and dismal; it was one of the last soggy days of the fall. The day seemed all the more depressing because of the winter about to imprison us. The prospect of irritable small children, snowsuits, boots, and snow didn't seem as far away as we wished. The group began to talk almost idly of the children and how on some days it seems so hard even to like them.

"Why? I always thought that it was going to be so easy and so natural to be a mother. Why is it so hard some days?" someone wondered.

"Maybe because the kids are around all the time. It's hard to have someone around *all* the time."

"They demand things from me all day long. Do this; do that; do the other thing."

"They whine."

"They fuss."

"They cry."

"They have to be dressed or undressed all the time."

"They're hungry all day long, and they hate everything I make them."

"They mess up whatever it is I cleaned up."

"They're obnoxious."

"I never get away from them."

"They hate me."

"They love me."

"They call me 'Mom, Mom, Mom' every second."

Kandy looked belligerent and a little sad as she spoke, "Sometimes in the morning I wake up, and I get thinking about all that, and I don't even want to get out of bed. I know what it's going to be like, and I just lie there dreading it."

"I know," Kathy agreed. "That's part of why I sleep in instead of getting up."

"And once I get up anyway and make her breakfast, she wants something else no matter what I make. I'd like to stir her little face in that hot cereal by the time she says she doesn't want it," Ruth added.

"You know I wonder how in the world I can get so mad at them so fast in the morning," Kandy said. "Sometimes they haven't been up for more than ten minutes when I blow up. Now I know. I lie there in bed thinking about how miserable they're going to make me when they get up and resenting them so much that I'm furious at them before they even get up. It's no wonder I blow up so soon—I've been stewing about it for hours. I think now that I know that, I'll make myself either get up sooner or not think about them before they're up. That way I won't be stewing, and I can also have some nicer time before they get up."

The group continued to try to take formless feelings and put them into words to give some shape to them. By giving them some definition, those hazy feelings could be looked at and seen for what they were—legitimate feelings with some response choices. We brought forward and shared places of individual discomfort and guilt to be healed, understood, changed, or accepted.

"You know, part of what I feel so guilty about is that when one of the kids asks me to do something or even when he comes barging in on me, I don't mind. But when the other one does that same thing, it drives me wild, and I'm all over him."

"I know. I don't care what they say. It's impossible to love all the kids the same. I have my favorite, and I know it."

"Yes, so do I. But I feel terrible about it. He gets away with murder, and I don't even care. I think he's so cute. But let one of the others try that same thing, and POW."

"When you put it that way, I don't think I like either of mine. I love them. I guess I must, or I would leave them, but I don't like them. They're a job. I guess I hate them more than I love them."

"Maybe your hate is on top and easier to recognize; maybe it's also more familiar."

"For me, if it weren't for him, I could make it very well."

"I only hate one of my kids, but I'm better now. I don't hate him as much as I did."

"You know Alcoholics Anonymous has a big advantage over Parents Anonymous. At AA they get to give up booze. In PA we have to keep the kids," Mary quipped. The laughter sounded good.

"The other night my husband decided he'd like to give us all up. He woke me up to tell me that he hated me. He said, 'I hate my family, and I hate your family, and I even hate you because you're *my* family.' Nice way to wake up, huh?"

"What did you say? What did you do?"

"I tried not to take it personally." Mary said ruefully, "I tried to remember that it was *his* problem, but I felt guilty. And then the kids woke up, and it was awful."

"Kids make everything worse."

"That's right. No matter what's going on, at the slightest hint of a fight or anything like that, they're right there. They're like sharks who get all excited at the smell of blood and want to kill."

"Or do you think they might come to protect you and stop your fight?"

"They do seem to pick up on my moods. When I'm bad, they're worse."

"Do you think they really pick it up from us, their moods I mean? Am I *that* bad?"

"I've read that *our* emotions are supposed to make them the way *they* are."

"I don't believe that, though. They're people, too; they aren't just little mirrors. I can be in a very good mood, and they'll still be in a bad mood. They have their own moods; they don't need mine."

"I think my moods make them worse, but I can tell you, plenty of times their moods make mine a hell of a lot worse too. So it's only fair."

"When my kids get crabby, I don't know what to do. I can't stand any of us."

"Really, when I can't stand them, it's because *I'm* in a bad way. And when *I'm* in a bad way, it's really *me* I can't stand. So then do you think when I can't stand them, it's really me I can't stand and not them at all?"

"That makes sense to me. I feel that way, too. Maybe that's why I'm down on them so often, because I'm down on me so often. How can I feel good about them if I can't feel good about myself? How can I do it?"

Inability to feel good about one's self was indeed one of the recurring themes that everyone understood, identified with, and took turns trying to overcome. On this day, Rosemary offered support.

"When you can't feel good about yourself, that's the time to lean on other people for help. That's the time to rely on other people's feelings. I'm telling you now that we like you, and we feel good about you. So the next time you can't feel good about yourself, don't even try. Just hang onto the fact that *we* feel good about you. And then call one of us, and we'll tell you. I know that's hard, especially when you feel bad already. So if you can't call, just tape up a note on the refrigerator that says 'They like me.'"

"Speaking of liking yourself," Anna said, "I have something to tell you all. I'm on a diet now; and, what's more, this time I'm going to make it. I'm going to lose weight this time. Harvey brought me three pounds of chocolate turtles and two pounds of coconut creams last weekend, but I didn't touch them. It wasn't even hard this time."

"What's making the difference this time, Anna?" we asked.

"Well, I think it has something to do with what we were just talking about. I feel good about myself now. I think I can handle being attractive now, and I think I'm even worth it. When I didn't feel good about myself, I didn't think I deserved to look good, but now I do."

"Sounds like Harvey isn't quite so sure."

"You mean the candy? Yeah, he really is jealous, and I suppose he feels more secure when I look like this."

"How are you going to handle that?"

"Actually, I think that is his bag of, you-know-what-I-mean." Anna didn't swear easily, and we laughed because we knew what word she was stumbling over.

"*Shit,* Anna, say it—*shit,*" Vicki prompted her.

"No, you said it for me. Thanks. Anyway, that's what it is. I'll tell him I love him, and maybe I can be a little nicer to him, but right now I'm going to diet. Then I'll worry about the next part if he isn't able to handle it. One thing at a time."

Kathy said, "Isn't it strange how the very people who should support you the most are the first ones to give you grief? It's my family who are the hardest ones of all to deal with. They make me feel the worst. I did my hair this new way a couple of days ago because I felt kind of good and I wanted to celebrate. My sisters jumped all over me and made such a big fuss about how weird it looked. I sure felt awful when they finished with me, but as you see, I'm not going to let *them* decide how I'm going to wear *my* hair." We agreed with Kathy and applauded her independence and decision.

Kathy continued, "It was the same when I was little. My family didn't do much to support me then, either. In fact, they were the worst then, too. My dad told me he should have built me a trough to eat out of because I was so sloppy, and all my sisters always told me was how clumsy I was. I was never allowed to carry my own water to the table. I was never allowed to have milk anyway—they said I wasn't worth it. Do you know, to this day I don't drink milk? I pour it for my kids, but I never drink it myself. But lately I've been noticing things, like I *can* carry things, and I'm not *always* so clumsy. You guys keep telling me they weren't ALWAYS right, but that's hard for me to believe.

I'm beginning to, though. Now I know I can carry things. I can carry my own glass of water to the table! Eat your heart out, Dad! Next it'll be milk for me, even me. And then I was thinking about how stupid they always said I was. They said I shouldn't bother to read a book because I couldn't understand it, and I should stick to cartoons on TV because I couldn't understand anything else. But you know what? The other day I watched a program, a real program, on TV and I did understand it. Maybe I'm not so dumb after all. Isn't that great?"

Sometimes talking out problems isn't possible. Sometimes it's better to leave things alone. On one particular day, ten out of the eleven people present at our PA meeting had very serious problems, and the balance they had worked so hard through the week to achieve was precarious. Taking a chance on losing what little balance there was by talking about these problems didn't seem wise. This was a good time to be tender and low-key.

And so the conversation was quiet and gentle. We talked about how stress affects the different parts of the body, where stress is first felt in the body, where it finally centers, and what can help it. One person began to rub someone's neck; someone else began a back rub; and still another person began to do some stretching exercises. We were skirting the edges of involvement. The conversation touched fleetingly on Anna's caseworker, June. That was a safe dumping ground; she had caused trouble for Anna before.

Suddenly Vicki bolted out of her chair, strode to the blackboard, seized the chalk, and wrote in very large letters "FUCK JUNE." She turned to face us with one hand on her hip and the other one pointing the chalk at us. "This is it, guys. This is the 'fuck board.' Let's hear it."

The response was overwhelming. "Fuck housework; fuck husbands, fuck kids; fuck supermoms; fuck schedules; fuck shaving legs; fuck change; fuck pain; fuck mother-in-laws; fuck alcohol; fuck therapists; fuck public speaking; fuck the past; fuck the present; and fuck the future." It was magnificent. Vicki wrote across the board as long as there was room. Then she wrote diagonally on top of all the writing, then in small letters, then in large letters until every inch of that blackboard was covered with writing. Every thought, every frustration, every fear was up there somewhere. It was an artistic work of life. The group was cleansed, healed, and released. In twenty minutes, the entire group had been changed and freed.

Chapter 13
Not Everyone Was Helped

We soon discovered that there were parents we couldn't help as well as parents who didn't really want help. As the months passed, we met some parents who didn't need or want what we had to offer; we refused to continue to offer help to one parent who attended our meetings; and we failed to respond to one parent who came to us for help.

We talked to several parents who couldn't be helped. In their book *Helping the Battered Child and His Family,* Kempe and Helfer estimate that ten percent of abusive homes cannot be made safe for the children involved. Five percent of the parents are psychotic and mentally unfit to care for their children. Another five percent of the parents don't like one or more of their children. They never will like them, and they shouldn't be forced to live with them. In cases like these, both parents and children would be better off if they were separated.

Carl and Judy, father and daughter, were involved in sexual abuse. Now that this abuse has ended, they remember the past quite differently. Carl's memories indicate his lack of understanding.

"It was mostly when her mother was out. Sometimes, though, even when she was home, in the night I'd get out of my bed and go into Judy's room. I guess I did that a lot. It was so quiet in the house, and everyone was home but asleep. I did do that pretty much, I guess. It wasn't that her mother didn't know. She knew, the bitch. I don't know what she's talking about that she didn't know. We never talked about it. I mean we didn't have anything to say. What's there to say?

"Judy's a good kid. I wouldn't hurt her. She's my daughter; I love her. Doesn't she understand that? It wasn't so bad. She's making a big fuss about nothing. I mean, what's the harm? I don't have clap or nothing like that. So she's had a penis in her mouth and rear end a couple of times more than most kids her age—big deal! She's my daughter.

"It started a few years ago. I was laid off at the time, and her mother was working. Judy came home from school and went into her room. I went in a little later to teach her some things about sex. She was getting to the age when she ought to learn anyhow—she was almost nine then. She was getting to be a big girl; it was time she learned. So I showed her a few things boys might do to her. Then I told her to do some things to me. She didn't want to do that, the bitch. It was okay when I was doing it to her, but she didn't want to do it to me. I told her a few things that might happen to her if she didn't do it, and pretty fast she started doing it.

"That was the first time. Once she knew how, I used her pretty regular. She's my daughter; she's mine. Nobody is going to tell me what to do in my own house with my own kid. After the first few times, she was a pretty good sport. I mean, what's the big deal anyway? Lots of people do it."

Judy's remembrance of those sexually abusive incidents in her bedroom indicates the trauma she experienced.

"Every night I'd pray, *Not tonight, Lord. Don't let him come in tonight.* One time I locked my door. He said if I ever did that again, he'd show me a new thing to do with keys. He'd know I wanted to learn something new. I was always scared. I was scared when I went to bed and scared when I woke up. It was awful; it was disgusting. I'd wake up with him standing over me and his big thing sticking in my face. He said if I didn't do it for him, he'd knock my face so far in, nobody would even know it was a face. He'd have done it, too; I know he would.

"It was disgusting. I was sick to my stomach. He said if I ever threw up again, he'd stick it so far in my mouth, I'd never talk again.

"I ran away a lot, about seven times I think. But he said I'd never run far enough away from his thing; that his thing would get me anywhere. I'd get it even worse when I got back. He said he'd show me what I almost missed. He'd put it everywhere, all over me, in my mouth, in my ass, in my hole, everywhere all over my body. It was horrible. He said I was meeting it all over again and would have to meet it everywhere.

"I didn't know what to do. I told my mother one time, or at least I tried to. She cut me off. She said I was making it up, and it was my fault anyhow. When I got pregnant, she had to listen. But I still don't have anyone to talk to about this. I sure can't tell my friends. They'd think I'm awful. Lately people have been telling me it wasn't my fault, and maybe it wasn't. I sure hated it and didn't want it. But I feel awful dirty, like it was my fault. I can't sleep good. I can't remember when I slept good. I keep waking up with a jump, thinking, *He's here again; oh God, he's here again.*"

From the discussion our group had about sexual abuse and its effects on a child, it is clear that Judy is suffering trauma in her home. However, the effects of being removed from a home and the resultant trauma and pain of that are not minimized by people who have experienced it. Therefore, the judgment about whether or not the members of a family fall within the ten percent who should be separated permanently must be made carefully and thoughtfully. We should not be quick to judge those who might or might not fall into this category. Often, these children are never seen by society. They are taken home from the hospital and do not reappear until the day they begin kindergarten. They aren't the ones who are dressed and taken to the grocery store; they are left behind in the prisons of their homes. They aren't taken to the department store; they are tied to their beds. They aren't the ones whose parents scream at them in the movies; they are home alone. But when we do find a parent who does fall into this category by virtue of illness or desire, we should be respectful of his or her situation and make it possible for that parent to give up the child easily and quickly.

One parent who did not want help in remaining with her child was Lois, who called one day to tell her story.

"I called because I'm going to kill my baby. That's not fair to her, so if there's anything you can do about it, then do it. I mean it; I really do. I've been thinking about it for days, and now I'm ready to do it. I never did want her, and I was right.

"When I first got pregnant, I wanted to have an abortion, but my mother wouldn't let me have one. 'I'll help you take care of it; you can live here with me. I'll help you,' she said.

"Now how is she going to help me? She works all the time. She said, 'What you did was wrong, and now you're the one who should suffer for it, not the baby. It's not fair to the baby to kill it. You shouldn't kill unborn babies.' Well, she got her way. I didn't kill an unborn baby—but now I'm going to kill a newborn one.

"I just want to have a good time. I was in the ninth grade when I got pregnant, and I want to finish school and have fun with my friends. I like school. I don't like babies and especially not my baby. She's selfish, stupid, bad, and she hurt me when she came out—she hurt me bad. Now I'm going to hurt her worse than she hurt me."

Lois should be allowed to give up her child. Her pain and resentment promise misery and pain for both of them should they be forced to stay together. There are other parents in this book who might sound as if they should be separated from their children, such as Joe in Chapter 7. Joe's wife always loved that firstborn son, however, and did provide the child with love and warmth. The father also had the potential for loving the child.

Some of the people who came once to our PA meetings didn't come back a second time. They felt that they didn't need what we had to offer. Addie dropped out because she felt she didn't really need help. She described her situation to us and explained, "It's not my fault, and it's certainly not abuse. He's the one who's responsible for any hitting that goes on. He provokes and provokes until I give in and smack him a little. He begs me to beat him. Then he's happy; he quits bugging me for a while. He really wants me to hit him. He's the one who forces me into it. I don't lose control or anything like that. I know exactly what I'm doing. It doesn't affect me one way or the other. I just do it for him. He's the one who wants it."

June was frank about not being sure if she'd come back to PA. She had said she could come once—that was her agreement with herself—and so she did. She wanted us to know that if it weren't for her friend's sister, who was a member of PA, she wouldn't be here at all. But she was going to give us a chance.

"What do you do here anyway?" June asked.

All of us leaped in with answers. "We talk about feelings...figure out new ways to handle old problems...laugh a bit...get out of the house...cry...have a safe space for ourselves...learn something new about ourselves...learn something new about each other...learn more about our children...have a good time...learn to be a family...hear people say good things about us...say good things about others...find out what's really going on inside of us." Our words naturally meant more to us than they did to June, though; she wasn't impressed.

So we tried to help June acknowledge part of our common problem with abuse with the statement "One thing I now do with my children that I would like to stop doing is..." The group members began to answer, one by one. But when June's turn came, she wasn't interested in discussing her behavior. She wanted to tell us what her children did that she wished they'd stop doing. She told us story after story demonstrating how "bad" they were, especially the oldest one. She said she absolutely had to beat him; there wasn't any choice. Members gave her chances to talk about her guilt—she didn't have any; to discuss her uncertainty about what she was doing—she was certain; to show her love for her child—she didn't have any, she was just his mother; to describe her own childhood—it was rotten and her kids were luckier than she had

132

been; and to talk about her desire to be a better mother—she thought she *was* an excellent mother; she just needed better kids. Eventually we moved to another group problem. June didn't come back.

Sally stopped coming to our meetings because she didn't find what she needed at them. During her first time with us, she explained, "I've been in psychoanalysis every day for five years. A couple of months ago, I had to quit because I ran out of money. I think I was beginning to get somewhere, though. Now things are terrible at home, and I was wondering if this group might help me. Can I come to your meetings every week and will you help me talk about me?" We welcomed Sally and asked her to share her problem with us. She was especially sorry to be quitting psychoanalysis at that time because her older boy, Craig, who was seven, was about to be released from the hospital where he had been for months with an emotional problem. It wasn't his first hospitalization, and Sally knew how difficult it would be for them both when he came home. She didn't want to fall back into treating him in the same abusive way she had in the past. And she also wanted some help in dealing with the baby when Craig came home and they all had to readjust to another person in the house.

Sally talked a great deal during that first meeting. She helped people to pinpoint their feelings about and reasons for some very specific actions. Her questions about past associations were sometimes very illuminating. But we didn't get to deal with many problems during that meeting, and toward the end, we had to hurry to handle in even a cursory way the major ones members were facing that week—How was Kathy going to get Ricky out of her bed? How was Mary going to get the idea of ghosts out of Clyde's head? How was Lil going to get Greg to stop taking Gerald's toys? How was Anna going to tell her husband Harvey that she wasn't going to take that job that had been offered to her?

Sally felt we ought to talk about why Ricky was in Kathy's bed and what that *really* meant to each of them. Kathy said it really meant that he was wetting her bed instead of his own, and she wanted him out of her bed *now*.

Sally wondered if Mary had any idea of what the ghosts represented to Clyde and what he was saying about unseen threats and deep-seated insecurities. Mary only wanted to figure out a way to get away from him long enough to get the laundry from the washer to the dryer without his having a fit.

When Lil was wrestling with the toy issue and what to do with Greg and Gerald, Sally thought that we should talk about mother love, sibling rivalry, competition in the home and possible sexual rivalry for Lil in the boys' actions. Lil wanted to get Greg and Gerald to stop hitting each other before she hit both of them—and hard!

Anna really didn't want to examine Sally's insights about Anna's relationship with her father and the mirror and glass images reflected in her experiences. She was much more interested in finding the actual words she could use to tell Harvey that she was not going to take on another job. These words were important because if Anna didn't say the right words, Harvey would hit her or get furious at her and abuse the kids.

Sally told us afterward that she was going to have to dig up the money somehow to continue analysis because PA wasn't going to be right for her. She claimed that there wasn't enough time at PA to talk. She said that we talked too much about actions and not nearly enough about the reasons behind actions. She said that we talked too much about the kids, and that if we'd talk only about the parents, then the parents would understand themselves. Once they did that, she insisted, they'd be good parents. But Sally also wistfully observed that despite her five years of psychoanalysis, she still hit her child just as often as she had in the beginning. "It takes a long time," she said, and she hoped the solution was just one more session away. We hoped so, too.

Once our PA group had to ask a member to get help elsewhere. Beverly had come to us because she knew she needed help badly. She told us how bad life was for her three boys and how bad it was for her, too. She was scared—scared of her life and of herself, scared of her boys and of everything else. She was afraid she'd do or say the wrong thing or even that she'd do or say the *right* thing and then have to accept the burden of approval. She was afraid to say anything, and she was afraid to say nothing.

So Beverly asked questions. In fact, she asked the same question over and over again, but she didn't listen to the answers. "Why?" someone eventually asked her. "Why do you ask so many questions if you aren't going to listen to the answers?"

134

"Well," Beverly replied, "when I ask you questions, I know you're going to have to listen to me. And I know you're going to have to talk to me. But when I don't do that, I don't know if you'll talk to me, and I want you to talk to me."

We said that we'd talk to her anyway, with or without her questions. We said that in fact we'd be happier to talk to her if she didn't stop each meeting by asking so many questions. The week before, almost the entire meeting had been devoted to one of her questions, and even at the end she hadn't been sure if we had given her the "right" answer.

Beverly said she'd try to keep from repeating her questions, that she'd try to really listen to our answers, that she'd spend some time thinking about them. But as the weeks progressed, we didn't see any change in her behavior. It became obvious to us that we couldn't meet Beverly's needs. Since she was apparently relying on us for all of her help and support and since we weren't giving her what she needed, we felt that perhaps letting her stay with us was the worst thing we could do for her.

Finally our group decided that we needed to make a decision about Beverly. We decided that she would have to go for individual counseling at least four times before we would welcome her back into our PA group. This was the hardest decision we, as a group, had ever had to make, and we had very mixed feelings about it. If we were her only help and support, then we couldn't abandon her and her boys. We really ought to stay with her to help her. But it was obvious to us that she needed more than we could give.

We told Beverly that. We asked her to go for counseling, to go four times, and then to come back to PA. While we were talking about that with her, we also discussed the difficulty she was having in changing. "Bev, sometimes we look at you, and it looks as if you're on the brink of changing," one member commented. "We think you're going to do it, but then you don't. What happens? Why don't you?"

"I'm so afraid," Beverly answered, "I'm just so afraid. It's like I'm standing on the edge of this cliff, and I just can't jump off. I know it seems as if nothing could be worse than the way I am, and I believe that, too. But I still can't jump off. It's too scary for me." Then she told us she was pregnant again. We thought that she'd gotten pregnant so she wouldn't have to change, so she'd have an excuse *not* to change.

The baby is five weeks old now, and Beverly has yet to give him a name. To her, he isn't anyone; he isn't a person. How can *he* be a person when she isn't? What does it mean to be a person? It means, among other things, jumping off the cliff every now and then. Beverly's still clinging to the edge.

Frieda is another parent whose needs couldn't be met by our PA group. As a child, the only time Frieda received attention from her parents was when they were angry at her. Then they lavished attention on her by either yelling at her or beating her. Even though this was negative attention, Frieda enjoyed it. Like all children, she needed some kind of attention, and like all children, she was willing to settle for negative attention when nothing else was available.

Because the only times when people paid attention to Frieda were painful times, she grew to associate pain with caring. The two became inextricably linked in her mind. As an adult today, Frieda doesn't know how to accept caring if it isn't accompanied by pain.

Our PA group experienced a dilemma as Frieda attempted to manipulate us into her familiar pattern. She was always late to the meetings; her arrival would always break the flow of conversation. The formerly rapid exchange of ideas would grind to a halt.

At a typical meeting, Frieda began, "Would it be all right if I asked what you were talking about?" Her voice was so quiet that we could hardly hear her.

"No, that's OK," we assured her. Then someone told her what had gone on during the previous thirty minutes. Frieda wanted to talk about something we'd mentioned twenty minutes before. "Is it all right if I say something? If I give a suggestion?" she asked. We nodded more out of politeness than interest, and Frieda continued, "I don't know, but maybe this might work. It probably won't, but maybe. It worked for me once, but I don't suppose that means it will work for anyone else. Can I suggest something anyway?"

By the time Frieda got to her suggestion, all of us were fidgeting in our chairs. We wished she'd get on with it.

Frieda no sooner finished struggling with her first suggestion than she began to move her fingers back and forth, signifying that she was going to speak again. It seemed that a long time elapsed before she stopped preparing to speak and actually began. "I wonder—I hope it's all right if I say something. I hope no one will mind, but I do want to say something. Is it all right?" We all nodded again, this time a little tightly, and Frieda continued, "I know I'm always late. I hope it doesn't bother anyone." Frieda leaned forward as she said this; her voice trembled with the force of her emotions. She looked at each of us in turn and spoke very slowly, pausing between each word. Then she settled her gaze on one person and fixed that person with her eyes. "I hope it's okay with everyone," she repeated. "I hope it doesn't disrupt the meeting."

The person she had been looking at took Frieda's bait, leaned forward to confront her, and said, "Well, actually, yes, Frieda, it does disrupt the meeting. In fact, it disrupts it a lot."

Frieda smiled a small, sincere smile—her first real smile in the four weeks she had been coming to our meetings. A bit of color came into her cheeks, and her eyes brightened. She leaned back in her chair in anticipation.

The confronter continued, "It really is very difficult for the group when you come in late like this. It's impossible to tell you all we've said, and we really don't want to stop and go over it again. It breaks the train of thought. But actually it's even more than that, Frieda. When you don't come until we're well into the meeting," the PA member continued, "it makes me feel as though you have better things to do than to come to this meeting. It makes me feel that you're saying to us that we don't count to you as much as whatever else it is that you're doing."

These words added to Frieda's enjoyment of the situation. "I understand," she said. "Go on. Is there more?"

"Well, I guess that the only other thing I'd like to say is that it's your right to come whenever you want to come. You may come on time or half an hour late, or you may come five minutes before we break up. You're welcome here whenever you feel the need to be here."

Frieda suddenly looked as if she were a balloon that had been punctured. She slumped in her chair and the color and animation drained from her face. Valiantly she tried one more time to get the type of attention she had known as a child. She addressed the entire group and asked, "How about the rest of you? How do you feel? Doesn't it bother you?"

"It's okay with me whenever you come," someone responded.

"I know it's hard to be on time," someone else said.

"It'll get easier for you," she was assured.

"Come whenever you can."

"I had a hard time being on time at first, too," someone admitted.

"As long as you need this meeting, it's here for you," another member promised.

We'd lost Frieda. She was incapable of responding to this kind of attention, and she continued to arrive later and later at the meetings. And when it was obvious that no more confrontation was forthcoming, she stopped coming altogether.

Frieda had been accustomed to getting her needs met by pushing and pushing against people until they blew up at her and abused her just as her parents had. But our PA group was not going to allow that; we were not willing to be manipulated into exploding at her, into losing all our hard won control. Trying to cope with situations without losing our tempers was a primary aim of our group. Frieda made that very difficult, but we were determined not to feed into her abusive needs, and we were successful. Yet in meeting our own needs *not* to abuse, we failed to meet Frieda's needs. And we know that by failing to meet her needs, we failed to make life better for her family. We know that the abusive episodes which originally sent Frieda to PA continue and that her home is not a good place right now.

Regretfully, our PA group totally failed to respond to one person who came to us for help. When Ellen attended one of our meetings, we didn't do much to make her feel welcome. Our group had had twelve members during its first year, and we felt we couldn't meet people's needs if we had a larger membership. We took one new member in when one of the original members moved away; that had been eight months before. So, for a year and eight months, we hadn't had any new people at our weekly meetings except as invited guests.

And then Ellen appeared. When we came into the meeting room, she was sitting on the couch. We moved around getting coffee and tea and murmuring to each other, "Where did she come from?...Who brought her?...Is she staying?...Who told her about this meeting?...Who said she could come?" Sometimes our group doesn't have any spare energy, and sometimes it does. That week it didn't; what energy we had was needed for our own group. We knew that ahead of time. Mary had been busy on the telephone all week, and she had told me beforehand that everyone needed to talk, that the meeting was going to be very full.

138

Ellen was a very nice person, and at any other time we would have been delighted to know and to help her. But her presence at this time evoked jealousy, possessiveness, greed, and a general lack of warmth. It seemed as if not enough empathy, sympathy, and good will were available to go around, and here was someone asking us to stretch those resources even further. That seemed intolerable to us. So we didn't share our group or our time or our empathy very well that day, and we weren't surprised when Ellen didn't come back the following week. We were sheepish and embarrassed by our performance, and we had good reason to be. Ellen, we're sorry, and we apologize.

Chapter 14
Summer Brings Remembrance

We were at the beginning of summer. Because summer seemed to be a higher stress time than usual for both parents and children, we decided to meet twice a week during the summer months and to use each second meeting as an opportunity for strengthening our bodies. We decided to take Yoga lessons together. We had read that if the specific parts of the body that bore stress and anxiety were strengthened, better control of the emotions would follow, and stress might be better tolerated. It sounded possible and was certainly worth a try.

Our Yoga class was held in the basement of a local church. We had two instructors, a man and a woman, who showed us what to do and how to move. Because Wendy was pregnant, she had to have a special set of exercises. The instructor told us that Wendy would have a very nice and calm baby as a result of following this program. (And indeed, she does have a very nice baby boy.) Then Vicki and Kandy found that with their back problems, many of the exercises were impossible for them. However, there were many exercises we could do together, and so we began.

Dutifully we twisted and turned, bent and stretched to the best of our abilities. Our abilities were varied, of course, and many of the exercises were difficult for beginners to do well. This was the first time we as a group had been involved in a given task where individual capability and progress could be measured. Each of us had previously been working on individual tasks; now we were doing the same things together, and comparison was possible. We said it didn't matter how well we did the exercises; the only important thing was that we did them as well as we could. Because they didn't look as good as the instructors, though, several members felt that they were not doing well and quickly reverted to their old feelings of failure.

The next regular Friday meeting was strained as members waited to see if their performances had affected the group and their place in it. It hadn't, and we moved from embarrassment and preoccupation with ourselves to admiration of those who could do the exercises well and finally into nonchalant acceptance of the process rather than the product. That was very freeing.

Settling together into the other Yoga group effort—meditation—also took us a while. We didn't know quite what to expect as we began our first meditation session. The instructors led us through the exercises and then through the relaxation process. They chanted the chant they were using for us and then allowed us to slip into silence. Minutes passed before I became aware of a slight rustling sound moving through the room. It took me a few moments to realize that that rustling had been Mary leaving. I followed her as quickly as I could, but she was already out of sight. I found her by the sound of her gasping and crying. She had run down the steps, through the hall, and was now huddled into a very small and pathetic heap. She was crying almost hysterically and trembling violently. Her hands, covering her face, were drenched with tears and perspiration. I held her close as her body heaved and writhed. Slowly she began to relax a little. The shaking returned sporadically, as she went in and out of her "flashback." She was taking a trip back into a specific incident she had suffered as a child and had buried under years of forgetfulness. In her mind, she was once again a child living through that same terrifying, abusive experience. The horror of the time, her own helplessness, and the shock of what her parents had done to her had a staggering impact on Mary. She hadn't made a conscious decision to allow the memories to come forth, but here they were, and they were demanding recognition. They had to be dealt with. During this flashback, Mary experienced all the fright and pain and shame and grief she had felt as a child. For a time, the flashback incapacitated her.

Mary's body was soaked with perspiration by the time she was able to talk. She talked and cried until the story was out, the incident shared in all its ugliness. Once it was captured in words and shared, it began to lose some of its power over her.

The Yoga instructors had finished their session and had come looking for us. They found us outdoors and sat down to talk with us in the warmth of the sun. They tried to reassure Mary by explaining to her that the force of Yoga meditation can bring back bleak and unhappy memories from the past. Usually, though, they said, these flashbacks don't happen during the first meditation. Mary told them that she had experienced flashbacks before, and so the meditation wasn't totally responsible. "At least that's one more down," she sighed. "How many more can there be, though? I think I must have had a childhood a hundred years long. How can there have been time for so many bad things?"

Mary was only the first PA member of our group to have flashbacks. As other members discovered that they had strengths, capabilities, and support, they, too, began to be more honest about their childhoods and to allow themselves thoughts about the past that they hadn't been able to permit before. Most of the members had blocked out substantial parts of their own childhoods. Since they hadn't been able to deal with their lives as children, they had come up with an excellent coping device—forgetting.

Once the people in our group began to remember, there was something almost relaxed about them. Even with all the pain, the agony, and the shame, there was something strong, purposeful, and right about the process. Mary now talks of the painful times with a little more confidence and security than she felt in the beginning. "I don't know how to explain it; I hate it. It hurts so much, and I'm scared to death I won't be able to get it back together again. I hate not being able to function. But I'm feeling relieved that I'm handling the things I thought I couldn't handle. I'm doing it. I'll be awfully glad when it's over, though."

The force of the flashbacks can enervate a person for some time. The energy usually available for living needs to be rechanneled to internalize the experiences that are surfacing. The inability to cope well is usually short-lived, however. Afterwards, the person faces life with a new and a well-earned confidence.

The people who have not yet remembered the past pains of their childhood are usually nervous about it. They want to protect themselves from hurt. Even though they do not know specific details, they are aware that some very, very painful memories await them. They would prefer never to know what these memories are. They are encased in a fear that they can neither express nor acknowledge.

Flashbacks from the past surface quite naturally when they are not forced. Sometimes, they come as a result of one phone call; at other times, years of support and encouragement are needed to free the past. There seems to be an underlying integrity to the natural experience that can be trusted. However, the fear of the flashback experience becomes more specific and less general as the time for remembering comes closer. Vicki expressed the fear of many PA members during one meeting, "I can't remember. I won't remember. I don't want to ruin everything I have now. I don't want to remember. For the first time in my life, I have a decent relationship with my mother. We're at each other's fingernails now instead of at each other's throats. I don't want to wreck it. I don't want to remember. If I remember, I'll have to hate her, and I don't want to hate her. I love her too much to hate her now."

"But you won't hate her forever," Kandy assured her. "It won't take long. We'll help you get through it, and then you'll be on the other side. You can do it. I know; believe me, I know. If I can do it, anyone can do it. And it's worth it, really it is."

We don't need to remember each and every detail from the past, but we must learn to integrate the past with the present. Each of us must come to peace with his or her past. This is important if we are to live fully and productively in the present.

The middle weeks of our Yoga sessions were quiet and uneventful. More creativity seemed to be flowing than usual. Kandy wrote a poem; Vicki wrote a prayer; Mary wrote a poem/essay; and the rest of us continued easily and comfortably with relatively few upsets. Our last session was a bit more disruptive.

Anna had been very upset all week. She had been having a huge attack of guilt. She was deep into blaming and damning herself, and she hadn't been planning to come to the meeting at all. So when she did agree to come, we were pleased. She said that she didn't want to exercise and didn't dare meditate, but we were glad she had come anyway. She sat on a chair as we performed our exercises, but after a few minutes she gave a little hiccup and hurried from the room. Vicki went right behind her. She knew what Anna was feeling; she had had the same feelings, and she didn't want Anna to have to be alone with them.

The rest of us continued to stretch and bend as directed. Kandy's back was bothering her so much that day that she eventually gave up all pretense of exercising and sat watching for a while. She looked depressed, and then suddenly she bolted from the room and took a different direction from that which Anna had taken. Wendy jumped up and went after her. Vicki came back in and Mary left, but Vicki hadn't come to stay. She got her blanket and left again. Ruth came in late as Jody and I tried to pretend we didn't notice what was going on. Ruth did her warm-ups and joined us on the floor. I left as the meditation began and went to look for Anna, Vicki, Kandy, Wendy, and Mary.

I found Anna, Mary, and Vicki in the balcony of the sanctuary of the church. Both Mary and Vicki had their arms around Anna, who was crying. They were talking with her about guilt and love, trouble and happiness. Anna was speaking as I came in. "I think I know a lot more about guilt and trouble than I do about love and happiness, and that's just what I deserve." She looked up at the cross over the altar and addressed her next remarks to Jesus. "How can You let this go on? How can You let little babies and children get hurt? Why don't You get off that damn cross and come down here and help us? Don't You know we need You?"

Mary's arms tightened around her. "Of course He knows we need Him. Where do you think we came from? Don't you know God sent us all for each other? He gave us each other and this group for our help and support."

"That's right," Vicki agreed. "He doesn't have to get down off that cross. He already did that. Now He's using *us*."

The conversation turned to the group meditating back in the other room. "Should we go back in?" Anna asked.

"Well, it would be polite." Mary, as ever, was concerned about Pat, our instructor's, feelings.

"It's almost over."

"But she's trying to teach us something."

"Yeah, to be well-controlled and calm."

"I think we need more lessons." Anna giggled a little.

"She probably thinks so, too."

"She probably thinks we're a bunch of crazy ladies. That's what I'd think."

"Today's session reminded me of a bus, with people getting on and off and in and out and doors opening and closing all the time."

"Well, I'm sorry we were rude to her, but I think being out here with you, Anna, is a lot more important than Yoga lessons today."

"I think you're right. But poor Pat! What a terrible group to teach discipline and control to!"

We began to giggle like little children and then to laugh out loud. We tried to hush our voices because we were in a church, but we were too glad to be laughing instead of crying. Laughter born out of joy and love and friendship and relief was echoing through the sanctuary. Vicki said, "If I were God, I'd be glad about these sounds in this place. This is beautiful. Laughter with love in this place—this is perfect. What better use for a church!"

Chapter 15
Lying, Loving, and Christmas

Although the Yoga experience was a good one, it was also a disruptive one, so it was with a sigh of relief that we resumed our regular once-a-week meetings. We caught up with each other by starting the meeting with the statement "One situation I am not handling very well right now is. . . ." Each member of the group in turn completed the statement, and we shared our pain.

Kathy asked if we would spend some time with her on finding a solution to a problem she was having. Having a problem and wanting a solution aren't always synonymous, so when Kathy asked us to think about solutions, we were glad to work with her on them. We always learned something new ourselves whenever we worked seriously on the solutions to problems.

Kathy related her problem to us. Her son Ricky was hitting her, spitting at her, calling her names, and acting altogether hateful toward her both in public and in private. The group asked if she would like to role play the situation. She said no, she didn't think she had enough choices available to role play. All she felt like doing was crying. She didn't know what to do. So Mary went to the chalkboard, and we began to brainstorm. During a brainstorming session, the members toss ideas out into the open, and the person at the chalkboard writes them down. One of the rules of brainstorming is that no one can comment on any of the ideas. Not commenting was always hard because some of the suggestions sounded so good or so funny or so important. But we held to our rule of just suggesting, not commenting.

"Go ahead and cry."
"Ask him why he's doing that."
"Hold him tightly so he can't move."
"Take him for a walk."
"Put him to bed."
"Read him a story."
"Hit him back."
"Tell him you love him."
"Throw water on him."
"Tell him he's hurting you and you won't allow him to do that."
"Hug him."
"Put him up for adoption." At that suggestion there was silence for a moment and then laughter, loud laughter. One more secret thought had been shared and thereby robbed of its

mysterious power. Now it was just another suggestion.

By the time we were finished we had the fifty ideas we aim for in a brainstorming session. Kathy looked at the suggestions and decided that she was going to try to tell Ricky that she loved him the next time he acted that way. She said she was going to feel pretty silly doing that because she'd never done it before and didn't know how to do it. When someone pointed out that she probably felt pretty silly when he was hitting her anyway, she agreed she didn't have much to lose.

At the next week's meeting, Kathy reported her results. She said that the first time she had said she loved him, Ricky had looked shocked—but he had stopped hitting her. She said she had been shocked, too, but pleased that she had been able to say it and pleased that he had stopped his hitting. The next time she said she loved him, he told her that he loved her, too. He had never said that to her before, and she was ecstatic! She liked that interchange.

We began another meeting with the statement "One thing my child does which really gets to me is...." We quickly discovered that lying was a general problem. The members had tried to teach their children not to lie in the usual ways. The responses they had made to their children flowed out—"I don't care what you do, just tell me the truth about it and it'll be better. I won't be so mad.... If you lie to me, no matter what it's about, you'll get punished. If you tell the truth, it'll be okay.... I don't care how bad you were, just don't lie to me. That's worse." But the lying hadn't stopped.

We continued to try to think of ways to stop the lying, and at the same time, we worked on trying to understand the questions which surrounded this problem—Why was it that we had such a hard time being lied to? What was it about lying that we couldn't stand? How did it make us feel? What did it remind us of?

"I don't know. It just drives me crazy," Vicki said.

"Same with me," Anna agreed. "It drives me wild. It makes me want to fling them right up against the wall when they lie to me."

"I actually see red when they lie to me," Jody confessed. "I know when they're doing it, and I really see red all in front of my eyes."

"I can tell, too, when he's lying to me, or at least I think I can," Vicki maintained. "He stands right there in front of me, and he lies to me. That's when I just have to force myself away from him. I turn my back on him and walk away as fast as I can, while I still can."

"It's like the ultimate insult to me," Mary said.

Nods of agreement and understanding went around the circle. It was a general problem, not just the problem of the people who had brought it up. So we looked for a common trait, some clue as to how we might better fight our reaction. What had made us all respond to lying in such an emotional way?

"Anna, who lied to you when you were little? Did anyone lie to you?" I asked.

"Yes, my parents did. My parents lied to me. My entire childhood was full of lies, all lies. I used to think I was crazy because I wouldn't remember things the way my mother said. She'd say so positively that I did things I never did and said things I never said, but it never occurred to me that maybe *she* was wrong. I thought it was me, and I thought I really couldn't be trusted, just like she said, that I really was crazy. But that's not true. It's her, not me. I know that in my head, but I don't really feel it."

"And Vicki, how about you?"

"Same thing. Anna could've been describing my childhood when she was talking about hers. Shifting truth is all I ever knew as a kid. Now I can't stand it. I have to have the whole truth, and I have to have it all the time. I won't be lied to anymore. I knew things had been one way, but then my mother'd twist them around 'til I forgot how they'd really happened. She made everything sound different than it was. I couldn't control it, no matter what I said. She made it sound different. It was horrible. I won't be lied to anymore."

Vicki was emphatic, but she was also inaccurate. "Well, apparently you *will* be lied to," I insisted, "for in fact you *are* being lied to. The question now is 'How do you respond to being lied to?' "

"Not very well. I'm close to being out of control. I don't like the way I've been responding. But it doesn't seem to matter how I respond anyway. They don't care. They don't even listen to me anymore."

Mary joined in to echo the same feeling Vicki and Anna were expressing. "That's what really drives me crazy. When the kids don't listen to me, I go bananas."

Vicki agreed and added, "Whatever I say, they don't

listen anymore. They don't do what I tell them; they don't pay any attention to me. It's different around our house now, and sometimes I'm not all that sure it's progress. It used to be that I'd say 'March' and they'd march. Now it's different. Ever since I stopped beating them, they don't listen to me."

We had to laugh at Vicki's indignation, but what she was talking about was a big problem for many of our PA parents. When the old style of relating and disciplining stopped, the children no longer seemed to think they had to obey. The parents were stymied. They didn't know how else to enforce their orders, and they didn't want to resort to physical discipline until they were absolutely certain that they could control themselves while administering it. So, for a time, the children weren't listening and were getting away with a lot more than they had in the past. This phenomenon was happening in many of the families.

Mary shared with the group a positive attitude she held onto when her children ignored her. "I read somewhere that when children feel good enough to ignore their parents, that means they feel secure in their parents' love for them, that they know you won't withdraw your love from them, that they don't have to worry about it. So when Clyde and Betsy don't listen to me, I just tell myself how lucky I am that they feel so secure now."

Anna said, "When I was little, I *had* to listen to my parents. I never ever would have dreamed of talking back to them—I know what would have happened to me. I did *what* they said, *when* they said, and *how* they said. But while I was being so good and doing just what they said, I know what I was thinking. Believe me, my thoughts were horrid. When I went to live with Gramma, I respected her. I did what she wanted because I liked her and I respected her. I didn't have to do what she said; I had a choice. I want my kids to be nice to me, to listen to me because they *want* to, not because they *have* to."

Jody agreed with Anna's beliefs, but putting them into action was hard for her. "How do you handle it, though? I can't take it when they don't listen to me. It really gets to me. How do you handle your own feelings when they don't listen?"

As usual, Vicki had a strong answer. "I don't give them a chance not to listen. I just start straight in screaming at them. I figure I'm going to have to end up that way anyway, so I might as well start out that way and save us all some time."

Ruth looked a little wistful as she thought over the enormity of the problem. "I want them to listen to me and to do what I say, but I also want them to think for themselves. I never sassed my parents; I was a model child. Now I'm not saying that's good; heaven only knows what it's costing me today to make up for always being so good. I really am paying a price now, and I don't want my kids to have to do that. I want them to learn to think for themselves, to be people themselves and to have their own ideas. But sometimes it doesn't seem fair that I have to pay my own price and theirs, too. I have to struggle with my own problems and also put up with them learning to fight theirs. My parents really had it easy with me as a kid."

Mary, too, had been docile and obedient as a child. "My parents told me if I loved them, I would do what they wanted me to. Whenever I didn't do anything perfectly, they told me I didn't love them. I knew it wasn't true, but I couldn't convince them. Now I'm finding myself on the other side of that same coin. When my kids don't listen to me or don't do what I tell them to do, I think they don't love me and that they're proving to me they never did love me."

Lil's head bobbed up and down in agreement. "I feel the same way. When they're doing something wrong, I think they're doing it to me—to punish me, to get back at me. I keep asking them, 'Why are you doing this to me?' "

Vicki began to cry a little. "It's what *I* do to *them* that makes me feel so bad, though. How can they not take it personally all the time? And they don't, thank God. Yesterday Lenny and I were in the middle of one of our wars, or rather I was in the middle of one of *my* wars with *him*. Right in the middle of it, he raised his head and looked at me and said, 'Mom, I love you.' It really freaked me out. I mean how *can* he? I was hitting him and he loved me! It doesn't make sense. You know, a while ago, nothing could have reached me while I was doing that, but yesterday his words stopped me cold. Talk about love conquering all!"

Not long after this meeting, our group was faced with an entire season of love—the Christmas season. But, as everyone knows, there's a lot more to Christmas than pure and simple love. There's exhaustion and misery, poverty and cold, family demands and inadequate strength, memories and hopes, as well as mistletoe and holly.

The additional stresses and expectations of the holidays

were costing the group members a great deal in terms of energy. The extra energy required for shopping and decorating had to come from somewhere, and it was coming from the store of psychic resources they were using to cope calmly and efficiently with life, to respond lovingly to family and children.

The new calls coming in for help reflected this deeper and sadder time of the year. One very resigned voice began, "You know what Christmas meant to me as a kid? It meant I got hit with a pine branch instead of a belt for two weeks. That's what it meant. This morning, as I grabbed a branch and was hitting my kid, I realized what I was doing. I'm doing the same thing! It was that mixture of pine smell and pain. I don't want to be doing this. So here I am calling for help. I don't suppose there's any help, but I thought I'd call anyway."

Another person called in surprise and shock and growing fear. "It wasn't until I saw the Christmas tree appliquéd on the pillow that I realized it was Christmas and I was trying to smother her with a Christmas pillow. I also realized that I put a pillow over her face every day now. What if I really succeed and kill her some day?"

A woman called after years of emotional pain and said, "It was Christmas Eve when my father first raped me. I still feel that dryness, the pain, and how much it hurt. Every time I see a Christmas tree or hear Christmas music, I think of that and I feel it all over again. It wasn't the only time he did it—my God, it wasn't—but it was the first. I can't seem to shake it."

The Christmas season continued to be difficult for our group. Kandy explained her feelings. "I'm sad every year at this time. I don't want to be. I don't want it to be bad for the kids; but this year it's worse than ever. I can't even function. I just sit around; I can't seem to move. I think about what it was like for me as a kid. My birthday is in December, too. So with Christmas and my birthday, that month has always been important to me.

"My birthday comes first. Year after year I can remember lying awake the night before my birthday wondering if my dad was going to come home for it this year or if he would still be in a bar somewhere. I hoped and prayed that he'd remember and that he'd be sober, but he never did remember. It never worked out that way. I never had a birthday party because we never could plan on him being in good shape. He never made it home for a birthday dinner. We gave up waiting and ate late without him. I can still remember how everything tasted, thick and hot and kind of stale behind tears I was trying to hold back.

"Christmas was even worse. We would wait longer for him then because it was more important, but finally we'd go ahead and eat. Then we'd try to wait for him to come home to open the presents. He usually made that, but it was awfully late sometimes. Sometimes he couldn't open his own presents, and we'd have to do it for him. It was not a good time, that's for sure. Sometimes he'd get mad; then it was even worse.

"I was married in December too, and for that I was nervous that he wouldn't even show up and that we wouldn't be able to find him. But it worked out okay. We had to drag him out of the hotel bar to dance with the bride, but at least we found him.

"And that's why December is extra hard for me. It makes it doubly hard for me because I know how bad it was for me, and I want so much not to have it bad for the kids. But I make it bad for them by crying so much. I want them to remember good things about Christmas, the way it should be."

No wonder Kandy had such a hard time with Christmas. This was the first year she had ever admitted to her deep sorrow, however. In years past, she had forced herself to pretend that her painful memories didn't matter. But this year she was allowing herself to feel sadness for her lost Christmases. She was mourning her childhood, and that helped to heal her. She may need to spend some time each December mourning what she experienced and grieving for what she didn't have, but when she is finished with her grief, she can move into the holiday time as she did this year. After mourning it, she let the past go. She had the best Christmas ever, and so did her family.

For Anna, Christmases were different than they had been for Kandy. She explained, "It wasn't that my Christmases were so bad; it was just that they were so nothing. That's what hurts about Christmas for me. It was nothing— a few presents, always clothes, and that's all—no big meal, no fancy table, no cookies, no nothing. It was the same for my birthday—no cake, no party, no nothing. I didn't 'need' it, they said.

"It's going to be different for my family. It *is* different for my family. We have fancy things on the table—crystal wine glasses, a linen table cloth, fancy serving dishes, and all the silver—and a big celebration for every holiday. And every holiday I'm so tired I think I'll die, but it's worth it to me to be giving them that.

Ruth understood Anna's desire to make Christmas memorable. She said, "Christmas for me wasn't *bad* either. I was okay. It was Bill who never had much of a Christmas, and now I want to make it all up to him. I want to do all the things for him his family never did. I want to make the cookies and do the entertaining and the decorating and the singing. I want it to be a big deal for him.

"I end up so depressed I can hardly stand it. I get so tired, for one thing. And I'm sad it was so bad for him as a kid. I hate to think of that. Then I feel responsible to make it up, but I can't possibly do that. I feel so bad that I can't, that I have to take to the couch again and I just lie there."

Not everyone in our group celebrated Christmas, but we all seemed to be traumatized by it.

We decided to try to set some reasonable expectations and limits for Christmas so that people wouldn't crash during the holidays. We began by making a list of all the things we thought we should do, either because we wanted to do them or because someone else wanted us to or because we always had done them. We covered the blackboard with tiny writing: bake cookies . . . see Santa . . . decorate the house . . . be well-dressed . . . visit friends . . . celebrate the birth of Christ . . . shop . . . wrap presents . . . go to church . . . be sexually responsive . . . serve good meals . . . be festive and happy . . . keep the house clean . . . see the family more often . . . and on and on. One of the last items listed was "fight suicide." The silence that followed as we looked at those revealing words was heavy.

The next step was to try to select a few individual priority items from the huge list. We wanted to narrow down our expectations to a number each one of us might manage. But even that seemed to be too hard for most people. Anna said she wouldn't even try. She was going to do it all. "You'll be exhausted, you'll take it out on the kids . . . . No one will like it . . . . They'd rather have you than all those meals and decorations . . . . It won't be good for you."

"I don't know about all that," Anna admitted, "but I do know that I'm going to do it all. I always stay up all night at least four nights out of seven before Christmas anyway. That gives me a lot of extra time, and I'm going to try. I'll tell you what, though. I'll choose one to work on extra hard. I'll fight suicide this year harder than I ever have before. I'll agree to that."

As each person shared her priority choices for the season,

"fight suicide" was on every list. It was the most important task for each member of the group that year. To have verbalized the intention to fight suicide seemed to make it easier for each of them; to share the goal gave the group a sense of support and companionship.

When Christmas came, the preparations we had made as a group paid off. Mary had Christmas dinner for eighteen; Anna's house and table were beautiful, and she did stay up all night for four days during the week before Christmas. She had both her mother and her mother-in-law over for the day and even that went more smoothly than ever. Ruth never took to her couch in depression at any time, and Kathy's first Christmas without her husband was tolerable for her and her children. Throughout this stressful time, parents related to their children and to each other in positive though tired ways. And for the first time for many of these people, Christmas brought no abuse with it. It was indeed a time for rejoicing.

Chapter 16
The Children

I arrived early at one of the first meetings of the new year and went down to the children's room. As I waited for everyone to arrive, I thought about all the changes that had occurred for everyone in the warmth of this room.

Soon Kathy arrived with her three children. I thought about the first time I'd seen her. She'd had only two children at that time (since our group had begun, four babies had been born to members). Now she had a new baby, Donnie. Her daughter, Tracy, had captivated us all from the beginning. A tiny blonde, she was incredibly feminine and beautiful. What I remembered best about her was her solemn little face which never showed a smile. Now I watched her smile broadly at me and then the others as they came in. She seemed to be smiling much of the time now.

Her brother Ricky had not been good at communicating with words when he first came. Clenched fists and strident shouts had expressed all his feelings, and so I watched with pleasure as he ran up to one of his friends and began to tell him about a cartoon he had seen that morning.

Kathy was carrying Donnie as she came in. She was holding him close to her, and they both looked happy. I recalled her telling us that she'd never known how to hold a baby or how to burp one. No one had ever shown her how with her first two, so our group did when Donnie came along. The ones sitting closest to her showed her their favorite positions, and then we took turns holding both Donnie and Hank, Wendy's baby.

Hank was older than Donnie by three days. Wendy had gone into labor with him during one of our meetings. We had timed her contractions and called her doctor, her husband, and her parents. We had been with her while she spilled over into tears at the realization that this was really the time, and we'd cried our own tears as we watched her kiss her daughters and go off to deliver her baby. This baby was going to be born into a family well-supported with friends; life for this child would have a very positive beginning. A few weeks later, when Wendy wanted to talk about how to care for a circumcision, we took Donnie's and Hank's pants off to demonstrate. Those babies were very close to all of us.

Now Marty was coming down the hall—I could tell from the sound of his crying. A year ago, he wouldn't have cried aloud for anything. This was progress for him. I remembered walking beside him one day as we were entering the church. It had been a wet winter day with enough warmth in the air to melt some of the snow into slushy puddles in the parking lot. Marty had fallen on a ridge of snow, and his hands had plunged into a puddle of water and ice. Marty hadn't moved; he hadn't made a sound; he hadn't even taken his hands out or gotten up. He had remained perfectly still, almost frozen into that uncomfortable posture. I'd picked him up and tried to brush off his hands and his knees. Silently, he had just stood there for a moment and then walked off as quietly as he'd fallen. This year, he cried and screamed when he was physically hurt or when his feelings were hurt. This year, he expressed himself with security because he knew that people cared. I liked to hear Marty cry.

Michael, with no diaper on, came crawling through the door from the children's room where his mother had obviously been changing his pants, She had not yet completed this task, but Michael was ready to see what else was going on. The first time I had changed Michael's pants, I had wondered at the incredible stillness of his little body. The minute I had started to take off his pants, Michael had become perfectly still. Little arms and legs motionless, eyes glued to my face, he had remained passive and limp as I changed him. This year, he was neither passive nor limp, and he tried his best to scurry away from his mother to find more interesting things to do. He giggled as she came after him, picked him up, and carried him back out of sight to finish the job. He snuggled against her, still smiling, and she, too, looked amused. That was good to see.

Lenny came glaring and stamping into the room. His anger was strong and wild. No one was quite comfortable when he got that furious look on his face. His eyes darted around the room, looking for a likely target, and we knew that sooner or later he would erupt. For now, though, the childcare workers were content to move a bit closer to him and wait for the parents to leave for their meeting before beginning to work with him. We were all much more comfortable with Lenny now that we had been together long enough to see his tantrums decrease both in intensity and duration, and he was more comfortable with us. I watched him make a wide circle around me to avoid coming close to me.

Lenny's action made me conscious of how much less touching went on now between the children and the adults. At the same time, however, I knew that much more *natural* touching was being expressed among all of us. When we had first started meeting, some of the children had spent a great deal of time and energy kissing and hugging the adults and even the other children. They seemed to desire a large amount of physical attention. Now they might occasionally hug or kiss on passing or in response to someone else's hug or kiss, but for the most part, they appeared to have better things to do with their time. In general, all of the children seemed to have better things to do than to pay much attention to the adults.

At the beginning of our group history, play would instantly cease whenever the adults came into the children's room. The children would cluster around the adults, asking them how they were or crying or hanging onto their legs. They asked a thousand questions designed more to check up on Mommy or Daddy than to find out any needed information. Now, as the adults come into the room at the end of a meeting, the children begin to gather up their belongings and put the toys away. The next few minutes still seem chaotic, but there isn't the frenzied hysteria that there used to be at the beginnings of our meetings together months before. Collecting twenty-five children and their belongings into proper pairings and groupings is never going to be easy, but it's getting easier. The entire children's area seems quieter and calmer, reflecting the fact that the parents are quieter and calmer—not only here, but also at home.

As we began our meeting that day, I commented on a few of my observations to the parents, and we continued on that theme for part of the meeting. We began with the statement "Since I first came to PA, my child has changed the most in that...." The looks on the members' faces reflected their mixed feelings in thinking about their children and change. Remembering their own progress and that of their children was impossible without also remembering the past. Pride in the children's growth and change was mixed with pain and guilt.

Many of the PA parents learned at some time that their children needed some extra care. Just as the parents were finally achieving their own victories in parenting, they were devastated again by their children's needs. Kandy had just found out that her children needed more than she presently knew how to give them, and her emotional reaction to that news was a mixture of guilt, sorrow, and anger with each feeling surfacing in turn. Guilt surfaced first. Kandy felt so bad because she hadn't been perfect as a mother that she thought she ought to kill herself to punish herself and to get out of the children's way. And then she began to be very sad. Here she was, loving her children, trying to be a better mother, wanting to give them whatever they might need to be happier and healthier people; but who had done these things for her? When she was a child, why hadn't anyone cared enough to bother thinking about her? No one had ever loved her that much!

And then the anger erupted. *It wasn't fair, damn it.* She was working so hard on herself and on the kids. *It wasn't fair.* If someone had worked with her when she was a kid, if someone had loved her enough to bother, she'd be in better shape right now and she wouldn't have to be doing so much. She was having to do it all, and it really wasn't fair!

The other members not only shared the same feelings as Kandy but also reached the same conclusion. Fair or not—and they agreed it wasn't—they didn't want life to be as hard for their children as it had been for them. So they were willing to work twice as hard to develop as persons and as parents while allowing their children the inconvenient freedom to develop as persons themselves. The situation was a handful.

We began to talk of the changes that had taken place in members' children. Carole began. "Marty's changed the most in his playing. We have such a good time together. He really knows how to play with things now. I never had clay or finger paints or anything like that as a kid, and now he has them all and he knows what to do with them. He shows me what to do, and we play together all day long. I haven't done anything else in weeks. I don't even go to the store. I can hardly wait for him to get out of bed in the morning and teach me something new. We never ever had such a good time together. We've covered all our walls, not just with his paintings but with mine, too. It looks cool." By teaching her to play, Marty was giving Carole the childhood she had missed.

Playing was a painful subject for Vicki. "My kids have changed and so have I since I met you guys. Things are better in our family, but still not good. I've stopped the negative, but I can't seem to start the positive. I don't do bad things anymore, but I don't know how to do good things. It's like I'm stuck up here on a fencepost between positive and negative. I have nothing now. I'm scared I won't ever have anything. I don't like it up here." Vicki's pain had been apparent to us for some time. She was crying as she finished telling us what was worrying her

160

this week. This was the last time she would be with us during an entire meeting. Starting next week, she would be spending half of the meeting time down the hall with the child-care workers, learning from them how to interact with children in a positive way. We felt good about this turn of events, and we were sure that the experience would help Vicki. Our child-care workers were good teachers, and Vicki would be a good student. But Vicki was afraid that we might be wrong.

Kathy was proud that Ricky wasn't spending all night in her bed anymore. That was a big accomplishment for her. "Now it's just between 3 and 4 in the morning or whenever he sneaks in. I've had some time to myself, though, because I read to him before he goes to bed and then I put him to bed alone. That also means he now wets his own bed half the time instead of mine all the time. That's much better!"

And Mary was glad that Clyde wasn't quite so afraid of ghosts anymore. "I still have to be on the same floor with him, but I can be in the other room. I don't have to be right there where he can see me; it's enough if he can hear me. "And I think he's closer to God than he was before. It used to be that he'd only think of praying when things were bad. In the middle of a crisis, he'd say, 'Let's ask Jesus to help us now, Mommy.' Now he thinks of giving thanks when things are good, too. And when I get uptight, he brings me the phone and tells me to call someone."

Ruth said she felt that she was more relaxed all the time and that the kids were better as a result. "I don't expect either Gail or Billy to be good all the time now, and I don't expect me to be able to handle them perfectly all the time, either. So now when they're bad—or when I am—I just don't let it get to me the way it did. The kids seem to be a lot more fun this way."

Jody smiled, but her pain was evident through her smile. It was very hard for her to talk about her children. On the day when we had had a child psychologist come to talk to the group, she hadn't even been able to come into the meeting. She had sat in her car while her children had played in their meeting room. Today Jody confessed, "I just don't want to think about what a bad job I've done. But I guess you can all see how Jonathan's changed. Remember how I used to carry him in with his blanket, and then he would lie in the corner for most of the meeting? Now he plays with the other kids most of the time."

Rosemary said, "It's their attitude I like the best. They're learning to know that sometimes it's other people's fault when things go badly, it's not always their fault. The other day we were in a store, and some lady started yelling at Tommy for something he hadn't even done. I started to talk to him about it, and he just said to me, 'Don't worry, Mommy. That lady just had a very bad day. It wasn't my fault.' I think it's really great that he can do that, that he can think about it from someone else's side instead of automatically assuming everything that happens is always because of him. That'll do him a lot of good in his adult years."

Anna said, "For me, the change I see in Ned is the way he responds to a compliment from me. I couldn't ever say anything nice to him before, but now I can. I can't always look right at him when I say it; I don't always mean it; but now I can say straight to Ned the same kinds of things I say to the other kids. Maybe that's not exactly *his* change, but it's what comes to mind right now."

Kandy looked pleased as she said, "For Sarah and Tim it's their ability to be with adults. Being with Dave and Betty down in the child-care room every week has really made a big difference in their attitude about adults in general. They're much more comfortable with them now."

Lil said, "The thing that's the most different for them and for me, too, is our temper tantrums. It used to be that when they started kicking and screaming, that's just what I did. I got right down there on the floor and did it, too. I couldn't control myself any better than they could control themselves. But little by little, I stopped. I learned to call another adult and to talk like an adult to an adult. I learned that I didn't have to have a tantrum, too; that I could stay an adult. And then they learned they had a choice, too. How could they learn anything different if that's all they saw? And how could I learn anything different if that's all I knew?"

For the most part, PA people haven't had much of a chance to learn anything better than abuse or inappropriate behavior from their own childhoods. It is in PA that they are learning to handle life in a more positive way. Life is now better for their children, who are learning at a young age the skills and techniques they need for handling their feelings in constructive and positive ways. Their parents are having to learn these skills as adults, and that's harder, but their children's lives are going to be less desperate than theirs have been.

Chapter 17
Sharing Our Growth

After a time of focusing on our own group, our own problems, and our own process, reaching out to others became important to us. Each member could remember very well what life was like before he or she joined PA, and now each one wanted other people to find the same support and help she or he had found. We began to think of and talk about ways in which we might be able to spread the message. Members first began to talk about telling their own families; this was important because of the sad fact that abuse runs in families. Each PA member had cousins, sisters, brothers, in-laws, and other relatives who would benefit from PA membership.

Mary was the first to tell a family member about PA. She shared the results of her revelation with us at the next meeting. "Well, the secret's out," Mary told us. "I told Denny's sister, Karen, that I belong to PA. I told her what we are, what we try to do, and why we're here. I emphasized that my yelling at the kids so much can be bad for them. I told her about verbal and emotional abuse and explained what we do together, how we help each other cope with problems, and how we call for help. I really thought she was understanding me and what I was saying.

"I guess I was wrong, though. She told Denny's parents, and we were supposed to go over there for supper last week. I was a little nervous, but I figured there wasn't anything I could do about it. So I just went. It was even worse than I'd thought. They all looked at me like I was a loony person or a criminal or both. My mother-in-law took Clyde and then Betsy off into the corner and asked them, 'Did mommy hurt you today?' Then she took off all their clothes and looked all over them for bruises. Thank goodness they haven't been outside on the swings much lately.

"The next day she came over to our house. She never comes over to our house, but she just sort of dropped by and took off their clothes again. Every day since then, she's done that."

We asked Mary how she'd been handling this. She replied, "Actually, I don't really know. It's kind of like a dream, more like a nightmare. I keep thinking, *This can't be real. This isn't actually happening.* But it is. Denny was furious with me for telling. He says he has enough problems now as it is. Well, he's right, I know. But it's done now, and they know. It's so absurd, though, with her dropping over every day and making up a different excuse to take their clothes off. It's ridiculous."

Mary talked to her own parents about her involvement in PA with very different results. The first hurdle for Mary to overcome was the fact that her parents wouldn't admit to any of the abuse she herself remembered so clearly. That nearly stopped her right there, but eventually Mary talked about the beatings her grandfather had given her. That memory seemed to be less threatening for her parents, and because she knew that her mother must also have been beaten by him, Mary was able to identify and finally talk with her mother about this abuse. Her mother admitted that she'd suffered severe abuse from her family.

Once her parents acknowledged that her grandfather had been a child abuser, talking about themselves as abusers became easier. Mary expressed her sympathy for the anger, shame, and guilt that they as parents must have felt. She explained that she knew those feelings so intimately because she had experienced them with her own children—she had known the same love and the same inability to handle anger constructively. Mary became the first person in either of her parent's lives to express any sympathy for what they as parents must have gone through. They received forgiveness and acceptance from the person they had hurt the most.

Mary told them of her desire to have a more honest and complete relationship with them. They were skeptical—they weren't sure exactly what she meant or how to achieve this new relationship—but they did agree to listen to her. Now Mary is helping her parents learn to express their own emotions in more constructive and healthy ways. She is talking with them about needs and wants and feelings they have always had but have never known how to label or talk about. Her parents are delighted with this new way of thinking and talking and seem to be having a wonderful time discovering a whole new world. They're delighted when they remember and when they want to exert the energy required to stay out of their lifelong patterns of poor communication and poor relating. Life is very different for that family today.

According to Mary, her husband is next. She says that he's a beautiful person, that he deserves a better emotional life, and that he can learn a new and healthier way of relating to people. She may very well be right.

Kandy had also tried to tell someone about PA and what it has done for her. "I was about ready to tell my pediatrician about PA last month," Kandy said. "I had it all set in my mind. I wanted him to know so that if he meets other people who need PA, he'll know what to tell them. I brought in some of the yellow flyers and literature, and I was all set.

"He put Kelly up on the table and started to look at her. Her shins were all black and blue and her knees looked terrible. (She's been learning to ride her bike, and she's a mess.) Anyway, he looked at her and said jokingly, 'I see Mommy's been beating you again this week, huh?' And he laughed a little at how ridiculous that was. I groaned inside and thought, *Nope, not this week. Maybe next week.*

"So this month I was ready again, but I wasn't sure I was going to do it. I made Bob go with me for support just in case I decided to go ahead with it.

"I did tell the doctor, and he seemed really interested. I gave him the flyers, and he said he was going to recommend PA to people. Then he wrote about PA on my chart. I didn't know he was doing that, but Bob saw it and told me later that's what he was doing. Does that mean the next time one of the kids gets hurt I'm going to get raced off to jail?"

Jody was quick to say, "No, but it might mean that the next time somebody needs help, he'll know what to say and who to call."

Mary still cringes when she remembers her attempt to explain PA to her children's doctor. She recounted the incident to us. "I finally got around to telling him. I started with my feelings about how I didn't always feel just wonderful about my children—I was starting small. I went around and around, and then finally I told him I was a member of PA. He said, wasn't that for abusive parents? Yes, I told him, it was. I told him there are lots of kinds of abuse, and it isn't all physical.

"I don't know what he thought he was doing, but he sure wasn't making it any easier for me. He just looked at me all the while I was talking; and then he said, 'That's impossible.'

"I didn't know what to say, so I just said, 'Oh?' He said yeah, that because I had nursed my children, I couldn't have a problem with abuse. I kind of laughed and said, 'I don't know about all that, but I do know about one thing. I need PA.' He kept saying I couldn't be one of THOSE, and I kept saying I *was* one of THOSE. Finally I think he believed me. But, boy, did his attitude change. He could hardly get me out of his office fast enough.

"The next time I came back, he had ordered some huge

textbook type book for me about child abuse. Either he forgot to mention it to me, or he was too embarrassed to bring it up; but in any event, he didn't give the book to me himself. He had his nurse bring it out to me while I was getting the coats on the kids. She looked at the title of the book; and she said in this real excited voice, 'Oh, are you one of THOSE?'

"I thought I'd die, but I just said, 'Well, yeah, I guess I am.' All the while she was staring at Clyde, who had his arm in a cast from falling down our steps.

"I wanted to say something, to try to explain, to get her to understand, but the phone rang. I waited around for about twenty minutes. The kids started fussing, so I had to leave. I felt so rotten. Around that time I said in a meeting that I'd never ever talk about PA again, that it wasn't worth it, that it was too terrible, that I was mortified. Do you remember?

"That whole next day was really terrible for me. I was really down about it. I was going to call that nurse, but I didn't. And then that afternoon the phone rang. It was you, Bee, remember? I'll never forget that. You said you needed to talk to someone and that the doctor had given you my name and said you could call me."

Mary and Bee both smiled as Bee picked up the story. "I really did need to talk, and he sure wasn't much help, as you know from your time with him, Mary. I had to work so hard to get your name, it wasn't funny. I told him I was in trouble, that I could do something bad, that I *did* do something bad, that I needed help, that I wasn't managing with my son. He kept telling me I was doing fine. I wanted to hit him. I guess that would have shown him. Here I was telling him I needed help, and he was telling me I didn't. I mean, where does he get his nerve?

"Finally he started mumbling something about some place where I didn't belong because I wasn't one of THEM. I had to practically beg him to tell me what he was talking about, and finally he told me something about PA. He said I didn't need that for sure, but I just about screamed with delight that there was a place that could help me. I told him I *did* need that; I *was* one of THOSE people; that was exactly what I was and exactly what I needed. Then he finally gave me your number, and I couldn't get out of there fast enough to call you up and talk to you. I never felt so good in my whole life as I did when I talked to you."

Mary said, "I felt pretty good, too, when you called. Somehow it made it all worthwhile, and weren't we funny when we both laughed and cried together?"

Kathy said she felt grateful because finding out about PA had been so easy for her. "I'm glad I have a different doctor. My doctor is the one who told me about PA. So whoever told him, no matter how hard it was for that person, it was really good for me. He was so casual and natural about it. He just told me that I deserved a little extra help and that PA would be a good place to get it. So I called the number he gave me, and here I am. So, to whoever told my doctor, thanks. You really made a difference to me!"

Besides telling our families and our pediatricians, we also began to tell the general public. It was obvious to us that a great many people were in much better shape because of involvement in a PA group. We had all found hope and help in PA, but many others needed that same message of hope and help. We wanted to share our discovery. So some members decided to accept some invitations to be interviewed. Vicki was one of the first to be interviewed for TV. Before the interview, she confessed her fears about it to our group. "The one thing that makes me nervous is the awful image we have. I hate to show up as a 'child abuser' when the whole world thinks we're green-eyed monsters. I should get a mask, a horrible ugly mask, and show up in that. I can say that's how they all think of us; and then I will take off the mask and reveal ME! A person, just a person. I'll talk about how PA is a place where you can take off your mask and become your own beautiful person, a person so beautiful you don't even need a mask."

Vicki decided to do the first interview quietly, and she asked to be filmed in shadow, more for her family's sake than for her own. She didn't want her family to be embarrassed by seeing her there or hearing what she might say about her own background. This filming technique was effective; Vicki wasn't recognized. The interviewer was fairly knowledgeable about the subject, and Vicki spoke well. She gave her own history and experiences and then, in response to a question from the interviewer, she began to talk about her feelings about being left by her husband. "When my husband walked out on me, I was alone. I had no one to turn to, no one to help me, no one to support me. I was trying to take care of the kids and deal with myself at the same time. And I was mad. I was mad at my old man for walking out on his kids, for turning his back on me and the kids. I was mad at him—I guess I still am."

Vicki had never verbalized her anger at her ex-husband for leaving his children, and it was a new discovery for her. Since that time our PA group has discovered that almost every speech or interview has brought with it a new insight or a new learning for the speaker.

Afterward, though, Vicki was a wreck. To appear anywhere as a "child abuser" took a lot of guts. She wanted to get the message about PA out, and she did. The experience was both exhausting and exhilarating for her. Two days passed before she felt like herself again.

Mary's interview also went well. She chose to be filmed in shadow for the same reason—her family. She said it wouldn't matter to *her* if she were recognized but her husband had a job, and they both had relatives. Her interviewer seemed to be sensitive and in tune with what she was saying. He wondered if he could film a small part of our PA group meeting to show how and where it was that changes could take place. He promised that no one would be identified except those who agreed to be filmed full-faced, and we agreed to the filming. It seemed to be a good time to try.

We were apprehensive the day of the filming. This was the first time we would be identified as a PA group before the public eye. We were uncomfortable and nervous about being filmed. The producer reassured us, and we reassured one another that it was going to go well. It did go well; the meeting was a good one: the people interacted well, the subject matter was interesting and productive, and we all had a good time. We were pleased and proud. We had risked ourselves in public.

As the night approached for the airing of the filmed meeting, members told friends and neighbors to watch and families gathered to see our debut. To our surprise and horror, the film began with slides of dead and battered babies taken from the Coroner's office. The message of help and hope was totally lost in the sensationalism of those gruesome pictures. The message that we had worked so hard to get across—that abuse wasn't always physical—was lost. We wanted people to realize that child abuse victims don't always end up in morgues. Our message of available help was lost in the horror of those slides.

The group was wildly and understandably upset. Each of us felt that the TV station had violated us and had raped our

168

personal integrity as well as the integrity of the group. We were outraged and injured; each person responded with every bit of energy he or she had. Anna called Mary because Mary's interview had been shown immediately after the slides, and Anna wanted to support Mary. Denny answered the phone and said that Mary had run out of the house crying and he didn't know where she was. "I do know that wherever she is, she's in bad shape," he said. Then Anna tried to call Vicki, but Vicki's line was busy. So was Kathy's. Apparently the two of them were talking. By this time Anna was desperate, so she went out, got into her car, and drove to Mary's house. Jody drove to Ruth's because Ruth's phone was tied up, and she gave her husband, Phil, strict instructions to call Denny every ten minutes to see if Mary had returned. Mary did come back, but she left immediately to drive to Kandy's so they could both go to Anna's. Anna was already on her way to Mary's—but they didn't know that. Bob was having another drink and trying to be patient when Kandy bolted out of the house to get into Mary's car. Jody and Rosemary decided that they, too, had better go to Mary's, so they took Jody's car.

Finally, they all ended up at Mary's house, where they stayed until dawn. They talked out their feelings about the show, made creative plans for revenge, dreamed dreams of the future, and reminisced about the past. By morning they all felt tired, close to one another, mutually supportive, and somewhat healed.

The harm done to the trust level of the group was severe, and for quite a while after that, we were careful about interviews. We limited them to personal appearances where we could control the content and to radio interviews where no one could identify who was being interviewed.

Eventually we reached the point where we were once again willing to risk a TV appearance. TV was a good way to reach people, and we had the opportunity to work with an interviewer who, we had been assured, was not going to violate us and would respect our story. So we agreed to be filmed again.

We had invited a guest sponsor who had been involved with PA for a number of years to be with our group during the filming. The meeting began routinely. We had the usual new triumphs, problems, and resolutions to be shared. We then began to move into individual problems, and Vicki was the first to speak.

Sometimes Vicki can talk for quite a while without paying much attention to what she is saying. She forgets to listen to herself, and she becomes uninvolved. Tom, our guest, became impatient. "What is this with all this head talk?" he barked. "You just started feeding everything through your head, and I got turned off. Can't you talk to me from your gut? I don't want to hear your head talk."

Vicki looked down and began to cry very softly.

"You're even *crying* from your head! For Christ's sake, don't you ever just plain *feel*? Don't you ever let it come out from your gut?" he demanded.

"I don't know," Vicki sobbed. "I'll have to think about that."

"You'll have to think about that! Even that! For Christ's sake, I'll bet you have to think about it before you go to the bathroom."

"Yeah, I do kind of play around with the idea for a while." Vicki smiled a little as she acknowledged this.

"Well, if you're going to talk to me," Tom insisted, "you're not going to think about it. I want you to talk to me from your gut. In fact, I *demand* that you talk to me from your gut."

"I don't know how to," she wailed.

Then Mary began to cry, too. Her crying sounded different—higher pitched, scared, desperately controlled. "You can't just *demand* that she do it," Mary cried. "*Show* her how. You have to show her how. Don't you understand? We know what you want us to do, but we don't know how to do it!"

Anna was getting angry at Tom too, and she broke in. "Stop it! You stop hurting her! You're hurting her! Stop it!"

Other members of the group burst in with expressions of their concern. "Does it hurt, Vicki?. . .Are you okay?. . .Do you want some help?. . .Where does it hurt?. . .Show us, Vicki, where does it hurt?"

"All over," Vicki finally said.

Tom took Vicki in his arms and began to rock her back and forth as he talked to her and to the group. Mary was crying harder now, and her body was tense even as it trembled. She was hunched up in her chair with her legs close together and her knees drawn up toward her chin. Kandy put her arms around Mary, but Mary still cried and continued to beg Tom to stop. "Stop it. You're hurting her. Stop it," she cried.

"I'm not hurting her," he replied. "I'm hurting *you*. Say it,

Mary. It's you I'm hurting. You're not crying for her; you're crying for *you*. You're the one who hurts."

"No, I want you to stop hurting Vicki."

"Am I hurting you, Vicki?"

"No," Vicki responded.

"How are you feeling?"

"Loved. I feel loved." As Vicki said this, Anna and Mary looked at each other and shared in their look the betrayal they felt. Vicki was feeling loved, and they had been certain that she was being hurt. Vicki liked being the center of attention even though that attention seemed negative to the others. This feeling reached back into her childhood; she had preferred to be abused by her parents than to be ignored by them.

Mary's and Anna's childhood responses to abusive attention from their parents had been different. They had preferred being left alone to being hurt. As adults they didn't want to be hurt anymore at all and would go to great lengths to avoid it if they could.

Vicki, Mary, and Anna reacted to this situation in their usual ways—Vicki enjoyed the attention, and Mary and Anna tried to avoid it. These two styles were obvious in their daily actions. Vicki's ability to be comfortable with attention focused on her made her one of the group's better confronters. She didn't mind putting other people in the "hot seat" because she didn't mind being there herself. Anna and Mary confronted other people in the group softly, by allowing them the space to confront themselves. Because this approach made them comfortable, they used it on others.

Anna's anger was now so great that she tried to confront Tom, but she couldn't quite get started.

"Anna, what would you like to do to me?" he said to her.

That was exactly what Anna needed—permission and opportunity to tell Tom what she'd like to do. She spit each word through her teeth at him. "I'd like to stomp on your toe!" she yelled. (Anna says now that she could give a much better and more descriptive answer if she were asked that question today, but that was what came to mind then!)

After a few seconds of silence, the group began to hum with congratulations.

"YOU DID IT. ANNA, YOU GOT ANGRY!"

"MARY, YOU FINALLY GOT ANGRY. YOU GOT ANGRY AND YOU LET IT SHOW!"

The group exploded with variations of congratulations. Both Anna and Mary had gotten angry; both Anna and Mary had been raised to believe that anger was bad. They had been punished whenever *they* had gotten angry and beaten whenever their parents had gotten angry. They had learned well that they *should* never feel anger. They knew for themselves that when they did get angry, people got hurt. This time, though, they had gotten angry; they had expressed it; and no one seemed to be hurt.

Two people were hurt, though—Mary and Anna. Mary spent the night on the telephone with the Suicide Prevention people trying not to give in to her wish to kill herself. In Mary's experience, anger was only supposed to hurt one person— herself. And so she turned her anger inward, first to depression and then to thoughts of suicide. The stronger the anger she felt toward someone else was, the stronger the need to punish herself grew. The experience with Tom during the interview had provoked a very strong feeling of anger.

Anna was physically sick to her stomach for over a week. She vomited several times a day, and she still develops severe nausea when she remembers the experience. Being angry and out of control actually makes her sick to her stomach.

The price that Mary and Anna paid for getting angry and expressing their anger was substantial. They are stronger and more confident people today as a result, but the experience was very difficult for them, and they still relive the pain they felt at the time. They're involved in a complicated process; they must learn to express constructively the very emotion they've been brought up to believe they shouldn't even have and certainly shouldn't express. And to make matters worse, anger is the emotion that gives them the most trouble with their children and causes them the most pain when they express it inappropriately or don't channel its release.

Yet, although this meeting had traumatic effects for at least two of the PA members, the show this time turned out to be well done, sensitive, and powerful. We were both relieved and pleased.

Not all of the people associated with PA were either relieved or pleased about PA much of the time. Husbands in particular had trouble relating to their PA wives as the women changed and got busier, more independent, and happier. So it was with some fear and much trepidation that we asked Denny,

Mary's husband, to present PA from a husband's point of view to our first city-wide meeting. We were nervous, but his voice was calm and relaxed as he began to speak. "It's been eight months since my wife got involved in PA, and I can tell you that I've really learned a lot in that time. One of the first things I learned was that in PA you cut the crap. PA is not the place for B.S., and so I'm not going to stand up here and B.S. you all. Now, if you're sitting there waiting for me to say all sorts of nice things about PA, you'll have a long wait. I'm not going to talk about how wonderful PA is because for one thing I'm not always so sure PA is wonderful. And I'll tell you why I think that.

"It was a few years ago that my wife told me she was having problems dealing with the kids. Well, I wasn't thrilled. I wasn't even tolerant. As a matter of fact, I was hassled and aggravated. I work sixty hours a week, and she tells me she's having trouble with the kids. I don't need that. I have enough. I mean, how tough can it be? They're kids, and she's an adult. I told her to get her shit together and shut up.

"So then she decided she'd read some books. I think she's read every goddamned book in the world about how to raise kids. One thing I've learned from listening to her talk about all those books is that anyone who has time to write books about raising kids isn't raising kids. There isn't enough time to do both.

"That didn't help. She said she was scared that it was getting worse and she didn't know what to do. And I began to see for myself what she meant. Things were kind of tense around our house sometimes. But it got a little sticky right here because she wasn't doing anything I wasn't doing. So if she said she had a problem with child abuse, what did that mean about me? I didn't like that thought, so I'd smack her, proving in that way that I was stable and sane and she wasn't. Get it?

"Well, this went on for quite a while—her crying and saying she had a problem and was scared; me telling her to shut up and get hold of herself. Then we'd fight, and she'd cry. Things were getting worse and worse. She was crying a lot of the time, and she was getting sick, first one thing and then another. It wasn't easy for me to admit I wasn't going to be able to handle her problem for her, that I wasn't still Superman. I'm not always all that ready to have that big red 'S' ripped off my shirt.

"But finally something had to be done. I was ready for someone to help me take care of her. If someone else could take some of this grief, well, great. We were just going around in circles. So finally I said, 'Okay, get some help.'

"She said, great, she was going to call PA. I panicked. 'Oh, my God, not PA! Can't you go to the church?' I pleaded. She reminded me that she had gone to the church and how bad that had been. 'Can't you go to another church? A doctor, a shrink, anything but PA? That's for *child abusers*. You're not one of them.' Well, yeah, she said she was. She said that what she was doing to the kids wasn't right. Maybe it wasn't the kind of abuse you read about in the newspapers, but it was still abuse. And she talked about how she didn't have any problem from her physical bruises and breaks as a child, but it was the inside part that still hurt. That was even more serious.

"And you know what that meant to me? It meant that if *she* had a problem with abuse, then *I* had a problem with abuse. And I didn't want one! But the truth was that sometimes I'm harder on the kids than she is. It meant that I was going to have to find some time to look at what I was doing with the kids, and that wasn't convenient for me. So I hit her some more to get her to shut up, but she still kept wanting to join. Finally she did.

"And how do I like it now? Frankly, I still don't a lot of the time. In fact, I spend a lot of time damning you, PA. Because of you, my dinner is never on time anymore. Because of you, I can't even call to see when it might be ready because she's on the phone all the time. Damn you, PA. Because of you, my socks are never folded. My car used to sit in the driveway for weeks on end, and now it's never there anymore. I don't even know if I'd recognize it except from the back as she drives away in it. Damn you, PA. Because of you, my bed hasn't been made in days. And more than that, I say damn you, PA, because you've made me look a lot harder at what I'm doing. I've had to face up to some things I'd rather not face up to right now.

"And my wife is changing because of you, PA. That's not convenient for me, PA, not convenient at all. I'm not sure I want this change. I don't always want to hear all these questions or talk about all these feelings. I really want to belt her some days. And she stands there so quietly and says, 'No, I'm a person. You can't do that to me anymore. I won't stand here for you to do that anymore.'

"Do you see who's taking it in the ear because of you, PA? It's me. It's not you, PA, it's me. It's *my* socks she can't fold; it's *my* dinner she doesn't have ready on time; it's *my* car she's driving around in. You'd think she'd take this and go dump it on her

174

parents. They're the ones who made her the way she is; they're the bastards who were so rotten to her to begin with. But does she? No way. It's me. It's not so convenient living with this person now. And so I say damn you, PA.

"But then I look at us, at our family. And there's no doubt about it—things are better. She looks better. She *is* better; she's hardly ever sick anymore. The kids look better. The house looks better—she's not home to mess it up anymore. She's more interesting to talk to, and we laugh together, too. And the kids, the kids don't cower when we get mad. Do you know what it's like to have a kid cower when you get mad? Well, they don't do that anymore.

"And so I say bless you, PA. We're better parents because of you, PA, and we have a better marriage because of you. Because of you, we're learning how to be a real family; and because of you, we're learning how to be real people. And so I say bless you, PA, because of what you've done for my family and because of what you've done for me."

Chapter 18
Learning about Our Feelings

Ruth looked tired but happy the day of the next meeting. "I had a rough night last night. I'd like to tell you about it because it was a victory for me. You know Bill's friend Bobby who just got married a few months ago? We were in the wedding, remember?"

Yes, we remembered. She'd missed a meeting because of the wedding, and we remembered when people missed meetings. Ruth continued, "Well, last night they came over after dinner. She looked just terrible with a big black eye and an ugly bruise on her cheek. Bill and Bobby went out to work on the cars. 'For God's sake, Barb, what happened to you?' I asked her.

"You know how I am when anything bad happens, or I see anything bad. I was almost sick to my stomach just looking at her. And then when she told me what happened, I was even sicker. He hit her, that's what happened.

"I couldn't even say anything to her. She went on to say that she didn't want to be mad at him, that she loved him, that she felt so guilty being mad at him. I said to her, 'For God's sake, Barb, you have every right to be mad at him. You *deserve* to be mad. You have a right to be mad!'

"Did you all hear that? *I* said she had a *right* to be mad! I finally understood. She *did* have a right to be mad. Nice people *can* get mad. It's not always bad and wrong to get mad.

"A victory for me!"

We all agreed. This had been a superb victory for Ruth, who had never really believed that the *feeling* of anger was okay. Because she felt she had to deny the feeling, she could only express it in explosions, not in choices. Mary had been following her train of thought and joined in congratulating her. "That's great, Ruth. That's really a great step for you. I know it's okay to be angry, at least for other people. I know it, but I can't do it myself. I don't know how to feel anger myself. But I think I'm getting better about it, maybe closer to it. At least other people's anger doesn't do me in like it used to. Last week Denny got mad at me. He was furious and yelling and screaming at me. But for the first time in my life I didn't automatically assume it was all *my* fault. I didn't start to tell him how sorry I was that he was mad at me. I told him he could be mad, but that it didn't mean it was my fault. This was the first time I even thought it might not'be my fault. I got my coat and stood by the door just in case I needed to make a quick getaway, but I didn't. He yelled, and I talked back, and it was great.

"Then we went over to his family's house for dinner. I started to help my mother-in-law with the supper. She said, 'No, never mind, I can do that myself. Don't do that.' She always says I don't have to help her, but then she turns around and complains that she has to do everything herself and no one ever helps her. Usually I just go ahead and help her anyway, and then she complains that I've done it all wrong and made more work for her. So this time, I just went back in the other room and sat down and talked to the people there. I had a good time. And when she started in after dinner about how no one ever helps her, I just let her talk and I didn't feel guilty.

"So I feel good today—tired, but good. Every time I make a big step forward like that, I'm exhausted afterwards. It takes a lot of energy to break old habits, even ways of thinking, but I'm doing it."

We began to talk about anger and how hard it is to handle it, to channel it so it's not directed at the wrong people, to deal with it emotionally. Kandy added her thoughts. "It used to be that when I got mad, I thought I was handling my anger when I stifled it down. I KNEW I WASN'T ALLOWED to get angry. But now I know that no matter what I *think* I'm allowed to do, I *do* get angry. The only real choice I have is what to do with the anger. Okay, I did learn that—with all your help. Then I learned to hit pillows and call you all, and I learned to cry and to work it through. I'm not nearly as afraid of my anger now; I know I can handle it if I pay attention to it. Now I want to do something about what makes me angry. I feel like I've worked on the symptoms, and I had to because that's what hurt people. So the way I express my anger isn't hurting them anymore, but I still want to work on the cause of that anger."

Mary had thought a lot about anger since her experience with Vicki and Mary and Tom at the TV filming. She agreed with Kandy and added her own feelings.

"I'm like that, too, but I never have any idea of why I'm mad until after I've blown up and said all I have to say. Then when I calm down, I see it was the same old things—guilt, insecurity, or fear. It really wasn't anger at all, but that's how it felt. So I try to keep working on those three feelings.

"I guess it's guilt the most, though—guilt when I don't do enough, guilt when I do too much, guilt, guilt, guilt. Then I explode and start all over again, feeling guilty about exploding from feeling guilty, and then I feel guilty that I spend too much time thinking about my guilt. HELP!"

Anna felt that she was in a dilemma, too. "I don't know how to help you, Mary," she said. "I don't even know how to help myself. In fact, things seem worse for our family now that I'm learning to express my anger than they did before. Before I used to explode every now and then, and that was terrible. The rest of the time I'd be quiet and terrified. I was always scared. But now I'm not scared, or at least not so scared, and I'm in no way quiet. In fact, I'm a bitch. I mouth off all the time. I let my family have it all the time about everything they do, especially Harvey—he gets it every time he opens his mouth. I hope this will go away, and it'll even out just like you said it would. Right now, he's not too pleased with me and my so-called progress. I really don't want to be like this, either."

Suddenly Lil leaned forward and said, "Well, I can't help you, Anna, and I can't help you either, Mary, but I sure do know what guilt feels like. In a way I kind of hang onto it, I know I do. For me, guilt keeps me from getting too happy. I don't deserve to be happy because of what I've done. So whenever I start feeling happy, I just make myself feel guilty again, and there goes the happiness—just like I deserve."

Kathy had found an easy answer as a teenager to stress and anger and guilt, but she had chosen not to keep living her life in that way. She told the group, "I never used to think about anything. Why bother? When I got uptight, I'd drink, and then I could do anything I wanted to do. I could cry and fight and everything else. Stuff I never did when I was sober, I could do when I was drunk. When I quit drinking, that's when I had to start learning to get in touch with my feelings and do something about them by myself. That was harder.

"It was much easier for me when I drank. I've always had the option to solve my problems that way, and a lot of my friends have been that way, too, and now here a lot of us are having trouble with our kids. I don't know what that means, but it must mean something.

"People say that drunks get drunk and do stuff they wouldn't do otherwise because of the alcohol. But that wasn't true in my case; I'd get drunk and do things I *couldn't* do otherwise. I was so sweet and quiet when I was sober, but let me get a drink, and boy, did I let it all out. I did all the things I really wanted to do all along. If it hadn't been for the kids, I hate to think where I'd be now."

Lil had some further insights into how people do certain things to enable them to act in ways they wanted to. "I think I kind of use losing my temper that way," Lil confessed. "I say I lose my temper and can't control myself, and then I do things I wouldn't want to do. But maybe I lose my temper so I can have an *excuse* to say and do the things I really want to say and do. No, it's not exactly that; I don't *want* to do and say those things, but I *do* want to feel better. And after I lose my temper, I feel better. It does work for that. What I really want, though, is to learn how to feel better without losing my temper and without hurting people."

Together the group acknowledged that one way in which most of them contemplated handling their feelings was to dream of running away. Escaping sounded like a good and clean way to get rid of a lot of confusion and demands. In the past, many of the parents had actually fled from one situation or another, and this temptation still influenced their thinking today.

Ruth had found a different release for her anger. She said, "For me, it's depression. When I get anything wrong, I get depressed and lie on the couch. I just stay there until all my bad feelings, no matter what they are, go away. If I lie there long enough, they do go away. But sometimes it takes a long time, and I don't want to live my life half spaced-out anymore. I want to experience real feelings, but I'm scared. I retreat the minute I get close to having any strong feelings."

Mary wasn't ready to talk about how she was dealing with anger—she wasn't even sure what anger *was*. All she knew was what she had learned as a child: that anger was not a nice feeling, and that if you showed it you were punished and beaten and sent to your room. She got so used to hiding her feelings that she forgot what it was like to release them. Recently, though, she'd been forced to become reacquainted with anger, and it frightened her. For the first time since her childhood, she had fully experienced the force of her anger, and its enormity had shocked her.

Nothing scared Mary more than being out of control, and she was certain that this new feeling was one she couldn't control if it happened again. She had been learning about her anger during the past few months, but that had been a gradual process: first she had been angry at the TV interviewer who showed the gruesome slides before our first TV showing, and then she'd been angry at Tom, and then at her husband. Her most recent experience of anger had come close to being an explosion, though, and she told us about it in detail.

"It all started in church," Mary said. "Betsy got down on the floor during the prayers. She was quiet for a while, but then she started moving around, so I thought I'd better stop her before things got out of hand. I reached down to haul her back into the pew. When she realized what I was trying to do, she scooted even further away from me. I was trying to take care of things quietly so nobody else would be bothered, and I forgot how fast Betsy can be when she puts her mind to it. I managed to grab her by the ankles as she headed toward the front of the church. She wouldn't budge, though, so I ended up giving her a tug, and then I pulled a little harder. She grabbed the closest thing she could find—which just so happened to be an older lady's leg. The lady screamed—I don't blame her for being surprised—and then Betsy screamed, too. I was still trying to pull her back up into the pew, but by now Betsy was mad and she wasn't going to have any part of it. I may have a problem expressing my anger, but she certainly doesn't! I knew that the whole church was in for it now.

"The next thing I knew, Betsy was running straight up the middle aisle. She got to the altar, grabbed the altar plate, threw it on the floor, and then ran between the priest's legs and went flying down the side aisle. I thought I'd die. By the time I finally caught up with her, she was at the back door, and the church service had come to a complete halt."

For Mary, the church service is the time and the place during the week where she soaks up her strength, cleanses herself from the last week, prepares herself for the next week, and luxuriates in the atmosphere of peace and prayers. Church is a sacred place and a sacred time for her. And Mary had been taught to act dignified and to be presentable in public at all times. "What will other people think?" was always in the back of her mind.

Her two-year-old daughter's behavior had ruined the peace of Sunday service for Mary and had put who knows what horrid thoughts in the minds of all those "other people." The combination of disappointment, shame, and guilt which churned inside of her gave rise to another very strong feeling. Looking at her daughter, Mary realized that she was experiencing a new, big feeling that she neither recognized nor liked.

Mary felt the physical effects of anger in her body—the tight muscles, clenched jaws, and perspiration in her armpits and on her skin. She had never before felt these physical sensations except when she was out of control. For her to be feeling this way without actually losing control was unfamiliar and frightening. She thought she was going crazy, and her first reaction was to want to sign herself into a hospital where someone else could control her.

The depth of Mary's anxiety was tremendous. Her strong programming against negative feelings was still very much a part of her. "Feeling this way isn't Christian," she told her husband. "How can I say I love God and still have bad feelings? If I have bad feelings, I don't love God, and I'll go to hell." As soon as she got home, she called her PA friends. These people—the ones she relied on the most—reassured her that what she was feeling was okay, that she was doing an excellent job of channeling her anger, and that they were proud of her. That night, Mary went to sleep and dreamed that she was imprisoned in a jail cell by guards who took turns raping her.

During the next PA meeting, the group turned toward Mary to try to help her make some order out of the internal chaos she was experiencing. She still wasn't sure that anger was the right name for it. "No," she said. "It's not anger. It doesn't feel like anger to me."

"What does it feel like?" we asked.

"I don't know how to explain it. I do know that it's big. It's as big as love and it takes over all of me. It's strong like love, but it isn't at all like love. It feels awful, not good at all. But it's so big, you have no idea of how big it is."

"You've never experienced overwhelming anger before, so how do you know this isn't anger?"

"This couldn't be," Mary insisted. "You all couldn't be talking about this. This is too big and too terrible. This couldn't be it. You couldn't sit here and talk about it so calmly if this is what it is."

"I think it is," Ruth said.

"Well, I don't like it at all." Mary trembled as she admitted this.

"And where is it written that you're supposed to like all your feelings?" Vicki asked.

"I don't know, but I do know that I was better off before I knew this feeling. At least then I liked my daughter. Honest to

God, right now I can't even have her in the room with me, I can't stand the sight of her. I'm scared of the way I feel about her. I don't even feel love for her anymore. I'm scared to be with her. I just want her to be somewhere else. I don't think she's safe with me right now."

Mary's words and feelings had been visibly affecting Kathy, who started to speak with a break in her voice and a lot of intense pain visible on her own face. "I don't know what you're saying. You mean you really hate her? You really honestly hate her? You can say that?"

Mary shrugged. "Right now, I can't say anything else. That's all I feel for her right now."

Kathy made a silent "o" with her mouth, and we waited for her thoughts. They weren't long in coming. "Sometimes I look at him, at Ricky, and I think I don't like the way he looks." She began to talk slowly and deliberately, but her words came more rapidly as she continued. "I think his face looks stupid; I think his face looks ugly. Sometimes I look at him, and he's ugly. My kid is ugly, I tell you." Her voice grew loud and hard. "I hate him! I hate that ugly kid!" She pressed her hand against her head as she leaned back in the chair. "I'm so dizzy. What's happening to me, you guys? What's going on? Am I cracking up? What's happening to me?"

"No, you're not cracking up," we reassured her.

Kandy spoke next. "What happened to you is that you said what's really on your mind. That's what it's all about. You were honest about your feelings, and that's hard to do. Especially if people think those feelings aren't very nice feelings. They're *your* feelings, though, and that's all they are. If you can say them, then they belong to you. But if you can't say them, then *you* belong to *them*."

"But isn't it awful to hate your own kid?" Kathy waited to be told how terrible she was.

"It depends," was the only response she got.

Then Anna spoke. "It's kind of like the first time you said, 'I love you,' to someone. You kind of got dizzy then, didn't you?"

"Not like this. I thought I was going to pass out a minute ago." Kathy still looked very pale.

Ruth had been quiet during this exchange, but when she finally joined in the conversation, it was clear that her thinking was very much along the same lines. "Now that you've said you hate him, Kathy, you can handle it. And the same for you, Mary.

It's when you *can't* say it that you can't handle it. Sometimes Bill comes home from work and I greet him at the door screaming at him, 'I hate these kids; I wish we'd never had kids. I hate both of them.' The first time I ever did that, he said, 'No, you don't.' I started right back in, 'Yes, I do. Don't tell me how I feel. My feelings are my own and I hate these kids. I know it won't last; it'll go away; but right now I'm telling you the truth—I hate these kids. You take care of them for a while. I'm going out.' It's when I *can't* say it, when I pretend that things are fine when they aren't, that's when I can't handle it."

Ruth was silent for a moment before continuing. "Okay, that's only part of what I was thinking; there's more. You know, it's funny about our feelings—we say we know they're okay, and we think it's okay to talk about them, but do we really know what that means? We all joined PA so we could get through some tough times without taking it out on the kids, without hitting them. Okay, so here we are. Mary, you've made it through a really rough week. It's been hell for you. But did you hurt her, did you hit her?"

"No, but I wanted to; I wanted to so badly."

"I don't care what you *wanted* to do—you didn't do it. And you, Kathy, he's been awful this entire week. I know, I've been talking to you. Did you hit him? Did you lose control?"

"No, but I said I hated him."

"You said that to *us*, not to *him*. You didn't *do* anything to him. Now, wouldn't you think we'd be sitting around cheering and carrying on about how great you both are? Are we? No! We're moaning and miserable and guilty and feeling rotten because our FEELINGS aren't always wonderful and loving. We don't DO anything, yet we make ourselves feel all kinds of guilt because of how we FEEL. Where will it all end?"

We looked at each other with guilt written all over our faces. Then Kathy began to speak. In a clear, small voice she said, "I don't know where it will end, but for now I feel a lot better. I don't have a headache for the first time in two weeks. It's all gone. And you know what else? I remember that he doesn't always look stupid. Sometimes he looks really cute to me, and I really love him a lot. Isn't it funny that by saying I hate him, I can remember I love him? It doesn't make sense."

Mary looked up and said, "I think I feel better, too. I went in and tried to touch Betsy last night while she was asleep. I figured I had to learn to touch her again, and it'd be easier to do it while she was asleep. I did it, but I didn't like it. But right now I feel like I'd like to hold her hand going up the stairs, and I think it's going to work. I know it is. I feel that little warm place inside me that's love for her again. It's back!"

Watching ourselves progress felt good, but we also needed to measure our forward movement and change; we had to have some clear understanding of where we were at the present time. During one of our next meetings, we decided to focus on the feelings which were causing the most problems for each person there. We planned to discuss our problems and feelings and then set some goals for ourselves. We used the question "What feeling is causing you the most trouble or pain right now?" to begin our discussion.

Lil offered with a smile, "It isn't trouble, but my big feeling this week is pride. I go around all day feeling proud of myself. Do you know why? Because I'm breaking the cycle of child abuse, *I'm breaking the cycle!* I really am. Last week proved to me what a long way I've come. Peter was having yogurt for lunch, and while I was in the other room, he smeared it all over that big mirror wall we have in the dining room. And I mean all over.

"I looked at him and I said to myself, *He loves me; he loves me.* I used to think he hated me and that's why he did it, to hurt me. But that's not true. And when I could think *he loves me* instead of *he hates me,* I didn't get so mad. I didn't have to hit him. He's not doing it to make me miserable.

"I looked at him and usually I would have seen this ugly-looking monster boy, but this time I just saw a little scared mixed-up boy. He's just a little boy.

"So I brought him a rag and I said, 'I know you didn't do this to make me mad, but you did do it; so now I'd like you to clean it up.' No yelling, no screaming, no hitting—and he did try to clean it up.

"Then all the while I was cleaning up after his cleaning up, I said to myself, *He loves me; he loves me; he loves me.* And then I knew I didn't have to hit him just because my mother didn't love me. He's not my mother; he's my little boy."

Lil's pride was cause for celebration, so we laughed and smiled and congratulated her and rejoiced for a few minutes. Then Mary continued. "I've been having negative feelings all week. I just don't like negative feelings, and I'm bothered when I have them."

Kathy said, "For me, the problem is that I still can't cry alone, and I need to cry. I have to wait until I get here to do it. I think I know you all can put me back together if I fall apart, and I can't do that myself, so I don't dare try to cry alone." After a pause, someone in the group suggested that she might try to cry on the telephone or ask someone to come over to be with her as she cried. Kathy agreed to ask two people over the next time she felt like crying. "That'll still be a group," she said, "but it'll be at my house, so then I can get used to it that way."

Anna had been having a really rough week. "I hate to say this, but you all know anyway—it's suicide thoughts for me again. It seems so right; everyone would be better off without me, especially my children. But I don't want to lay any more on them. I don't want them to feel rejected by my killing myself. Other than that, I feel like I'm right back to 'suicide summer.' " Groans from the group met her statement. We remembered "suicide summer" all too clearly. The temptation to self-destruct had moved with epidemic pace and devastating virulence throughout the group. I saw the looks the group members exchanged and knew that Anna wouldn't be alone this week.

Although most of our members were mothers, we did have the opportunity to welcome an occasional father to the group. James was new, and we could tell that he was worried about what we would all think about him. "I know I haven't been coming here long," James said, "and this is going to sound terrible, but the thing I've been worrying about all week is hitting Peter. That's my problem feeling."

"It's okay to talk about hitting Peter; it's not too terrible. Everyone here knows how you feel, and it's okay," we assured him. "But hitting isn't a feeling; hitting is an action. How do you *feel* when you hit him?"

"Like hitting him."

"What else do you feel when you hit him or even right after you hit him? What else do you feel?"

"Well, I guess I feel mad at him. That's one thing I feel," James admitted.

"Then that's the feeling you're having trouble with. Anger is the feeling; hitting is what you do with the feeling. The hitting comes after the feeling."

"It doesn't seem that way," James said.

"Maybe not." I said. "Maybe you're already hitting him before you notice that you feel angry, but the feeling does come first, and it comes from inside of you. Next time try to notice how you feel. If you can notice your feeling *before* you're hitting him, do. But if you can't, then notice it *while* you're hitting him. Then the next time you can notice it on the way to hitting him while your hand is still in the air. And then you can notice it BEFORE you hit him. Feelings are different from actions, and you can find that out for yourself. Feelings are always okay; actions aren't."

We continued around the group. The other members added fear, bitchiness, an overwhelming desire to leave home, hate, guilt, confusion, and helplessness to the list of problem feelings. Now we wanted to talk about what people were doing to minimize the feelings they'd expressed. Making the transition from problems to solutions took a few moments.

Mary began by saying, "I can't seem to plan out anything to try with my feelings. Or, rather, I can, but I always forget what it is when things get tough. I'm by nature a very spontaneous person. The other day I had a funny experience, though. Clyde had been being absolutely putrid; he had been into everything there was and had been beastly all day. Anyway, the crisis moment finally came, and I didn't think I'd be able to keep it all together. Before I knew what was happening, I grabbed his arms and yelled at him, 'You know what I'm going to do to you?' Then I was standing there holding his arms, wanting so badly to hurt him, but determined I wasn't going to do it. So you know what happened next? The next thing I knew, I found myself waving his arms up in the air and saying, 'Fly, Clyde, fly. We're going to fly all around the room. That's what I'm going to do to you.' It was terrific that I could find out that neat thing to do with him, and was I surprised! We must have looked a riot." The picture of Mary and her son Clyde flying around their living room made all of us laugh. Her spontaneous solution to anger had been a delightful one.

Wendy joined in, "I still use my 'emergency survival kit' idea. I keep that list pretty close to me now. Remember when we listed things that made us feel good? Well, I've added to it and now it's longer—call a friend...have a cup of tea...read a book...bake a cake...pray...go for a walk...watch TV. Nothing very earth-shattering, but that's okay. When I'm down, I just start at the top of the list and go down it one by one. By the time I get to the bottom, I usually feel a lot better."

Ruth turned to the group and confessed, "I'd need a list

about twelve miles long for that to work for me because when I get down, it takes weeks before I'm even halfway up again. But right now I'm finding I have some control over my feelings. For me, that's a new discovery. I guess I used to think that my feelings just kind of popped out of nowhere, made me miserable, made me do things I didn't want to do, and then disappeared just as mysteriously as they had appeared. It was like I was an innocent bystander, and they came and went as they pleased, doing with me whatever they wanted.

"Well, last weekend, I got a little bit of a new slant on it. We were having a family picnic for which I really wasn't in the mood, and I mean *really*. I was going to have to cook, pack the lunch, clean the kids, get everything organized, and then go off to be on my best behavior all day long. It was a dreadful prospect, and I was turning into a real bitch just thinking about it. So do you know what I did? I thought of this real neat person I know; her name's Debbie. She's fantastic—really a super person. I decided I was going to pretend I was her.

"So that's what I did. I smiled like she does; I talked like she does; I was organized like she is; I loved my kids like she loves hers; I did everything the way she does. I was even nice to my old aunt like she is. The really funny part about the whole thing is that I had a good time, and I wasn't panicky, and I didn't get flustered, and the kids didn't get to me. So now I know I can control some of how I feel by controlling how I act. And once I can act one way, I can feel a little differently—not a whole lot, but a little. That's good for me to know."

"What I'm trying to do is to make my feelings and my actions match the situation," Kandy said. "It seems to me that all my life I've either underreacted or overreacted. The tiniest little thing will set me off into hysterics, and then something big will come along and I won't even react. Now I want to learn how to measure situations, to make my actions match my feelings. If I'm feeling a little bit guilty about not babysitting for a friend, then I want to do something a little bit nice for her. If I'm feeling very guilty about doing or not doing something, then I want to do something big. I want to be able to scold the kids a little bit for doing something a little bit bad and then to really yell at them for doing something very bad. I want to be able to spank them and know I'll be okay. I want to make things match and come out balanced, but I don't quite know how."

"I'm feeling better about all my feelings now. I don't feel

quite as scared of them, and I'm trying to stop avoiding them," Vicki said. "I find it takes more energy for me to block out my feelings than it does for me to deal with them. The sooner I get into them, the sooner I get out of them, and the better off I am. But I also want to tell you that I'm still scared to death each time I start out. Scared that I won't make it, that I can't face it, that I'll begin to unravel everything and I won't be able to ravel it back up. I'm afraid that this time I'll go crazy. Even so, though, I still intend to battle them through. I try to figure out what it is I'm feeling, and sometimes the only way I can do that is to really get into whatever it is. Once I let it bloom inside of me, then I can tell what it is. *Then* I have some choices; then I can see some things to do. Or one of you can if I can't."

It was time for us to end our meeting. We cleaned up the coffee and tea, put the cups and the pot away for the next meeting, and went down the hall to get the children. As we walked, we finished up bits of conversations and then said our good-byes for that week.

"Have a good week."
"Call if you need anything."
"Give them hell at your speech on Monday."
"Keep me in your prayers."
"Don't screw around until you get that diaphragm."
"Let me know how he reacts to that new idea."
"Don't forget the book next week."
"Thanks for the cookies; they were great."
"Take care of yourself."
"I love you."
"See you next week."

Chapter 19
Epilogue: Hope for a New Beginning

"I'm so scared I don't know what to do. I feel like I'm falling apart, like I'm going crazy. I'm scared, really scared of what I feel like doing, of what I might do. She's been screaming for two days now. I didn't know babies could scream for so long. Nobody told me they could do that. She doesn't even sleep at night.

"I'm afraid. I've shaken her so hard I could've hurt her. I could do much worse than shake her, too. I can't get her to stop crying. The sound of it is driving me crazy. I have to do something, but I don't know what to do. I've rocked her and fed her and changed her and taken her outside, but she still cries and cries and cries. I'm really scared by how out of control I feel. I'm afraid I'm going to hurt her, really hurt her.

"You must think I'm some kind of monster. I think I am; I know I am. Who'd want to hurt a little baby? But I do. I can't help it—I do. Help me, please help me. I don't like how I feel.

"My husband tells me it's normal to feel this way. If this is normal, then I don't want to be normal.

"I know God means me to take good care of her. I'm letting Him down just like I let my mother and father down. It's the same story all over again. Now I'm letting my baby down.

"It's like I'm a big failure. I have this neon sign in my head flashing *failure, failure, failure.* All my life—failure, failure. I can't stand it any more. I'm so afraid of what I might do. Please help me!"

This was one person's call to PA. As Katy appealed for understanding and help, it was obvious that she was very frightened, both for herself and for her daughter.

It's different for her now. Since calling PA for the first time, she has worked very hard with her feelings, her thoughts, and her actions. She has waded through hours of tears and joy, facing old feelings and experiences, present realities, and future possibilities. She has struggled to get to where she is now, but she claims that she isn't finished working yet, that she isn't satisfied. She says it isn't enough that she's in control of her actions with her children. It isn't enough that she doesn't do the things she used to do and that she never did the things she feared she might do. It isn't enough that she's better; she wants to be better still.

Katy is very impatient. She asks, "Why, why? Why aren't I better yet? When will I be?"

"Katy, you're in such a hurry!" we tell her. "Relax. You can't undo twenty-nine years of experience and problem building in one short year. Relax."

"And what's going to happen to my children while I 'relax'?" she wants to know. "Don't you understand? I don't have time to relax! My children are only young for such a short time. I want to be better for them now. I don't have the luxury of a lot of time to relax."

She's right; it *is* important that she change. She *doesn't* have a lot of time, and neither do we. Every day in the life of a child is important. Every day affects the adult that child will become. Katy may not be able to make radical changes right away, but she will be able to begin making some changes quickly. Most abusive parents have enough energy and a desperate desire to enable them to change. PA can offer some techniques to divert the anger, and PA groups can provide the support that parents like Katy need.

Ninety percent of all abusive homes can be made safe; some of the parents may never have all of the patience or good humor possible, but their homes can be made emotionally and physically secure for their children. Most adults can learn to be good parents; they can learn to respond to their children in positive ways.

The real "experts," the parents who have abused their children, say that all parents want to be good parents. People who have been there claim that the ones who don't act as if they want to be good parents, who refuse to admit they have a problem, are indicating their own fears and insecurities rather than their true feelings. Abusers who have learned to deal with their problem also say that parents who act as if they don't want help do so simply because they don't have the energy they need to deal with the abusive situation or they don't know that help is available to them. It's not that they don't *want* help; rather, they don't know how to *use* help. It's hard to admit a need for help, especially in the area of parenting; too many people assume that parenting is a skill anyone can perform easily and perfectly with neither training nor help. Obviously, this isn't the case.

Most people truly want to parent well. Their intentions aren't the source of their trouble; their abilities (or lack of abilities) are. People who abuse their children don't differ from other people as much as their actions may lead us to think. They have the same feelings we do; they may express them differently, but the feelings are the same.

The parents in this book differ from other abusive

parents only in that they have called in for help. Their stories and their feelings are all too common. Their backgrounds are no better and no worse than those of parents who have not yet called for help. Their experiences are no less painful, their selves no less vulnerable, and their problems no less severe. They are the same mixture of fear and love and hate and insecurity and hope that all other parents are.

We know there are parents who abuse their children and have never called in for help. There are parents who abuse and don't feel it's wrong. They believe in the old maxim "Spare the rod, and spoil the child." For some of them, discipline means punishment. To many of us, their kind of punishment sounds like abuse.

When Charlie brought his ten-year-old son, Larry, to the hospital, Larry's back and buttocks were covered with welts, most of them healing well. The one or two that had not healed looked as if they were infected. The Emergency Room called the police, and Charlie was reported for child abuse. Charlie was a little surprised. "I didn't abuse him," he stoutly maintained. "I did beat him, though. He was smoking pot and ain't nobody in our family gonna do that no more. He knows the rules, and he knows what happens when he breaks the rules. I hit him with the belt, and I hit him until he was good and sorry he had done it, and he's decided that he ain't gonna do it no more. I think he ain't neither.

"My other two boys, I took the belt to them, too, when they was bad that way. And they didn't do it often neither. A couple a times, that's all it takes. I care about my kids, and I care that they don't do that no more. They're going to grow up good boys if I have to whup them from now 'til next Sunday. They know better than to be bad, and if they forget, well, I'm the one who's going to remind them." Charlie's older son, who had ridden along to the hospital, nodded and smiled in remembrance. He thought that his father made sense.

So what *is* abuse? Who is allowed to define it, to determine what it is and what it isn't? Where does punishment end and abuse begin? Whose value system can be used in making this crucial distinction?

The relationship between physical punishment and parenting styles is difficult to define. Every parent has the potential to find and use a valid parenting style that is right and good for that person and his or her child. However, parents who have had trouble with abuse have understandable difficulty believing that they can indeed be good parents. They have no faith in their abilities to parent well, nor have they much reason to have faith in those abilities. So far they haven't been very obvious.

The question of the validity of physical punishment is almost always raised by parents who are concerned with parenting. Cammie, a mother of two young children, had adamant views about spanking when she first came to PA. "I'd never spank my kids," Cammie insisted. "How am I going to teach them anything better, anything about love and respect, anything about discipline if I just hit them every time they do something wrong? If I go down and meet them on their level—the physical level—I demean myself, and I'm not going to do that. I'm going to reason with them and treat them like people, not animals. I don't want them to grow up like I did. I'm not going to fall into that pattern. But I lose patience with them all the time, and I scream so much. I lose control. That's not right, either."

A few months later she told us about some changes she had experienced. "You'll never guess what—I've finally learned to spank my kids! I think the reason I was giving them so many choices was because I didn't know what to do myself. I was making them make all their own decisions because I didn't trust myself to do it. We were all so confused, and they behaved horribly. Now I tell them, 'Here's your choice. If you want to behave like that, I'm going to smack your behind. Is it worth it to you?'

"You can't believe how much nicer our home is now that *I* tell them what to do. They still have plenty of chances to make their own decisions, but *I'm* the mother now."

This may seem rather simple and obvious to parents who are comfortable with demonstrating authority and taking responsibility, but it's extremely difficult for parents who have little self-respect and no role model of a good disciplinarian.

One of the factors that needs to be examined in attempting to solve the discipline/abuse conflict is the self-control of the parent. Is the parent in control or out of control when disciplining the child? The question of motivation must also be dealt with. Does the parent react to the child's behavior or to a need to vent his or her own feelings and relieve his or her own frustrations? Another consideration is whether

194

the demand made by the parent is legitimate for the child at his or her particular age. A three-month-old baby isn't capable of being toilet trained, yet babies of this age have been killed by parents who have become enraged because they felt that their babies were not cooperating. A ten-year-old *is* capable of making his or her bed and cleaning his or her room, however; these are age appropriate demands and expectations.

No matter how appropriate the demand may be, though, *no* misdeed excuses broken bones, burns, or other results of cruelty. But what about the parent who *was* in control, who *was* correcting the behavior of the child, and who *was* making an age appropriate demand, but who hit a little too hard or who by mistake hit in the wrong place?

What about people like Charlie? Charlie says that he's going to teach his kids "good sense and good manners." The rest, he believes, is up to them. He appears to be doing just that. Can we be so sure he's wrong?

The inability to define abuse adequately causes problems for the courts, the schools, and the medical and social service professions, but it doesn't really cause problems for the parents. The parents who are afraid that they are abusing their children don't ask what the criteria are; they know enough about the feeling. They find definition enough in their own lives, and the definition of abuse they give us describes a feeling they know all too well. Some of the incidents they classify as abuse—for example, one woman wanted to kill herself because she had called her two-year-old daughter a "bitch"—might seem minor to us until we start listening to how these parents feel, what they fear, and how they themselves were scarred by just such "minor" abuse themselves. One quickly learns that there is no such thing as minor child abuse, and that our definitions of child abuse have been much too narrow.

Each new telephone call to PA from a parent who feels that she or he has been abusive represents hours of torment and misery, hours of crisis, abuse, and regret for the parent and his or her child.

"I was beaten with the buckle end of a belt every day of my life, and I don't want that for my child. But sometimes I get so uptight I don't know what to do. When I found myself beating him with the belt, that was when I knew I was in trouble."

"It's like an addiction for me. Once I get started hitting

him, I can't stop. I just hit and hit and hit."

"I put a pillow over her face. Every single day since she was born, I wanted to smother her. Today I tried. You have to help me."

"I put my curling iron on her bare leg, and I watched her flesh blister. I did it three times."

"I say things to them I don't mean. I yell at them all day long. I really love my kids, but I yell at them so you'd never know it."

"I can't get my kids back unless I change. I don't know how."

"I'm not enjoying my kids. Sometimes I think I might hate them. Oh, the hell with it. I *do* hate them most of the time."

"When I look at her, I want to hit her. Every time I look at her, all I can think of is my fist in her face. I want to smash her. That's no way for a father to feel."

"I wanted to push him out in front of the car. I was holding his hand as we crossed the street. He didn't know I was more dangerous to him than any of those cars. They, at least, didn't want to hurt him. I did. I wanted them to run over him."

"I threw her on the bed a lot harder than I intended. When I saw her bounce so high, I knew I was out of control."

"I give and give and give. I do everything he tells me, and I don't even mind. Then he asks me for one more thing, and I explode. I'm all over him. I don't even know it's coming. What happens to me?"

"I hurt my daughter to get back at my husband. It's him I hate, and he hates it when I hurt her, so I do it on purpose. I need help."

"It was the scared look in his eyes when I came at him that got me. When I saw him look at me that way, I knew things were bad. I didn't even know I had a knife in my hand; I was just going to hit him. I do it so much it's almost routine. It wasn't until he started screaming like that that I remembered the knife. When I saw that knife, instead of wanting to hit him, I wanted to stab him, to kill him. My God, help me."

"He looks like my brother to me, and I hate my brother. So I hate my son. What can I do? Where can I put him? Or put me? I don't want to hurt him any more; I want him to be safe from me."

"I can't explain it, I don't understand it. I should be the happiest person in the world. My husband has a good job; we have plenty of money; I have a maid; we travel; I play a great game of tennis. But all I can do is hate myself because of what I do to him. I beat him more and more and harder and harder. If they ever find out, they'll take him away from me."

"I want a family, my own family. That's all I want. For as long as I can remember, I've wanted a family. A family with a mother and a father, a family with kids, a family that laughs and loves each other. My family was so bad when I was little. How I want a good family! I had kids, but that didn't work. They aren't my good family. Now I have six kids, and I don't have a daddy anymore for my family. I feel like killing them all, every one of them, and then starting over. Then I'll get my real family."

"I just don't know what to do or how to act. I've never been a mother before, and all I want is to do things right. But I was abused when I was little, and I know these things have a way of repeating themselves, so I thought that if I could get hooked up with some help right here in the hospital, then when I get home, if I think I can't manage, I'll know what to do."

"I love him so much, why do I do it? What kind of people are we that we have to hurt other people to make ourselves feel better? What kind of a person am I?"

Each call has the same basic underlying message: "I don't like how things are with my child and me. I don't like the way I feel or the way I act. I would hate more than anything else to hurt my child, but I'm afraid I might kill my child." Behind each call is a painful accumulation of tears, pain, and shame. Although these parents call in desperation, many have no real faith that there is any help for *them*.

Dawn is typical of many of the parents who call PA. She knows that she needs help, and she would like to come to the PA meetings, but she's afraid and full of excuses as a result. She won't leave her baby with a babysitter she doesn't trust; she doesn't know anyone she trusts; she's afraid the group won't help her; she doesn't want to talk about her problems with people she doesn't trust. She feels better talking on the telephone because she knows she can hang up any time she wants. During her first phone call, she admitted her confusion.

"My husband says I don't trust anyone. I don't know if he's right or not. Yeah, I do. He's right. I don't even trust you enough to tell you I don't trust you, but there it is. I don't know how to trust anymore.

"I used to trust people, at least a few people. It's been a

long time, though, since I was a kid. It was when I was a kid that my mother told me one day to get dressed and packed—I must have been four. She took me over to a home for kids that was near us. She always used to say she'd leave me there one day, and this day that's exactly what she did.

"I remember standing there with my bag of clothes in my hand, waiting for someone to come to the door. I watched my mother drive off, and I thought I'd never see her again. I was right—I never did see her again.

"I stayed in the children's home for a while, and then they started putting me in foster homes. Some of them were okay; most of them weren't. All in all, I was in fourteen different foster homes. I liked one of them. I was happy there. But I guess they didn't like me because they moved me on. I cried that time. Mostly I didn't cry, but that time I did. The rest of them weren't so good.

"In one of them, my foster father was real nice to me. That lasted about two weeks; then he raped me. He kept on doing it until finally I complained about it, and then I was the one who got blamed for it. He said I was asking for it. He said it was my fault. So I got put out of there, too.

"Then I started sleeping around with lots of guys. What difference did it make? I liked it when they'd hold me. I loved the feel of their arms around me, and I was willing to do anything to get that. What I did was get VD, and that was the end of my last foster home. I've been on my own ever since.

"Nobody's ever helped me do nothing. I don't know why I even called. You probably won't help either. Yes, I do know. I called because I love my kid and I treat him rotten."

During an initial phone call to PA, another parent told of how she had made the decision to trust.

"I have a terrible time with trust. I've never trusted anyone, not anyone. I learned early not to trust anyone. In my family, trust was stupid. You trust somebody, you get hurt. But the way it is now, I really don't have much of a choice. I can either choose to trust now, or I can wait until I have to take him to the hospital, and then the choice will be made for me. At least this way I can control who I talk to and where my son is while I get better. I have to trust. I have no choice."

Parents who call PA for help are trying to trust, and many succeed. First, they trust the person at the other end of the PA answering service. They trust the concern and the expertise of that person. They trust that the PA volunteer knows their pain and desperation and will help. If they come to a PA group meeting, they trust the sponsor and the members.

Most of the sponsors are professional social workers or psychologists. They have many reasons for volunteering to sponsor a PA group.

"I love the way groups of people work together. I love their potential, their caring, their experiences, their sharing. I want to enable them to work better together."

"I'm a protective service worker, and I see abusive parents every day. I'm always the bad guy, and I don't have the opportunity to see positive changes very often. I want to have a good experience in the field of child abuse."

"I like the idea that with a few hours of my time every week, I can make life better for twelve families all week long. That's really a trip for me."

"I know what I went through as a young mother, and I want to help make the family situation easier for other parents."

"I have some extra time now, and I'd like to do something worthwhile and enjoyable with it."

"It's one way I see that I can really live my ministry."

"I consider myself to have been an abused child, and now that I'm a psychologist, I'd like to use my training and skills to make life better for children today who are going through what I went through a long time ago."

Many professionals besides those who sponsor PA groups have a good understanding of the dynamics of child abuse, but many others don't. In their public speaking engagements, inservice training, and teaching seminars, both PA parents and concerned professionals have found that in many instances even professionals who are involved with child abuse don't seem to understand the phenomenon very well. During the past two years, professionals from various disciplines have made the following comments. The parents—the "experts" in the field—answer them.

From a pediatrician: "There's more child abuse today than there ever was before."
A. "Probably not. Certainly there aren't babies left on mountains or children in factories, but what's really different is our recognition of the rights of the child *not* to be abused."

From a minister: "Don't they *care* what they're doing to their children?"

A: "Yes, we care. We love our children, and we don't like hurting them."

From a social worker: "I'd never do a thing like that."

A: "Like what? Can you honestly say that you have never in any way abused a child? Not verbally or emotionally?"

From a congressman: "Those parents should be locked up."

A: "Then what would happen to our children? Will you take care of them? Is that the best thing for them? Wouldn't it be better for us all if we learned to take care of them well ourselves?"

From a psychiatrist: "They can't help it."

A: "In the past, we couldn't. Or, at least, we didn't. But we can *learn* to help it."

From a policeman: "Let *them* find out what it feels like. Beat them."

A: "We were beaten. That's where we learned what we know how to do now."

From another pediatrician: "They ought to be able to control themselves."

A: "We know that. We don't always know *how* to control ourselves."

From a third pediatrician: "Those kids don't deserve that. They have rights, too."

A: "We agree."

From a teacher: "They should know better. We should teach them before they have kids."

A: "Right on!"

From a clinic physician: "It's our fault for allowing poverty, unemployment, and poor housing."

A: "Yes, poverty, unemployment, and poor housing do make things harder, but there is more to it than that."

From a lawyer: "It's the court's fault. They let the kids go home too soon."
A: "Sometimes that's true. Sometimes we aren't as safe as we think we are. But other times, we are far safer than we fear."

From an obstetrician: "Women are the abusers. They do it more often than men."
A: "Only because women are home with the kids more of the time. When men are home with the kids as much as women are, they abuse as often. Abusive behavior is not a sex trait."

From another minister: "Men are worse."
A: "No, they aren't. But they are stronger, and so the consequences can be more severe."

From a judge: "What kind of a parent would beat a kid?"
A: "A parent who doesn't know what else to do."

From an emergency-room pediatrician: "They should be sterilized."
A: "That doesn't help the kids we already have."

From another social worker: "Those people really aren't so different."
A: "Yes, in a way that's true. But because we're hurting someone else, we *are* different."

From a protective services worker: "Some kids would be better off out of the home forever."
A: "Absolutely."

From another policeman: "If they can't take care of their kids any better than that, why did they have them to begin with?"
A: "We didn't know it would be like this."

From another lawyer: "It's mostly a low mentality, low socio-economic class problem."
A: "Not so at all, but more poor do get reported. Suburban doctors report less frequently."

From an audience of therapists treating child abusers: "What do you want from us as therapists and as people?"

A. "We want you to accept us, to understand us, and then to help us learn to be better parents."

To understand someone first requires listening to him or her. It's difficult to listen to people who have problems they can't talk about very easily. Thus far, we haven't made it easy for people to talk about their problems with child abuse. Many of the old social problems are no longer considered taboo topics of conversation, but child abuse is still unmentionable. The issue is further complicated by the fact that child abuse is illegal. We have condemned child abuse and child abusers and have made it almost impossible for the people who do need help to request it openly.

We all have the capacity to be child abusers. The feelings which lead people to abuse their children exist in each one of us. We can understand child abuse and the child abuser a little better if we can learn to admit to and own these feelings in ourselves. The people in this book should not be incomprehensible or inhuman to us; they are as ordinary and as extraordinary as we are.

We don't need to understand thoroughly the backgrounds of these parents and their present circumstances in order to respond to them. We don't need to know exactly what they mean by the words they use or why a particular parent communicates in a particular way. We don't have to diagnose all the symptoms and label the parents according to a psychiatric textbook before we can help them. Parents may disguise their pleas for help in generally hostile manners or in intellectually tiring trips through their heads—the nature of the disguise really doesn't matter. What *does* matter is whether or not we are sensitive enough to be aware of and respond to their request for help before a threatening situation escalates into tragedy for the family.

Parents who are abusing or who fear they may abuse need understanding more than anything else. They have ambivalent feelings about their children and ambivalent or predominantly negative feelings about their own performances as parents. Until someone understands what they're saying about themselves and the feelings they have about their parenting, parents who abuse will never be able to think or feel differently. They will be bound to the same thoughts or feelings until they are heard and respected for what they are saying. They don't need a lecture.

They may very well need some child-rearing education in the future, but they don't need it right away. What they need right away is our support in helping them to find alternatives to abuse.

People need other people to support them. A person's spouse may provide that support; however, the presence of a spouse doesn't preclude the kind of aloneness that can lead to child abuse. After months of loneliness and battering by her husband, Susan verbally and physically abused her children. Had someone recognized her cry of loneliness earlier and given her some warm, human empathy, she might never have struck out at her children. Finally, she contacted a PA group, and in the warmth of their support, she was able to relate her story. "I'm new here in town. I really haven't met anyone at all. This winter weather hasn't helped either. I don't have anyone to talk to. My husband is no help to me at all. In fact, he makes it worse. I think I might be better off without him. He's a compulsive gambler, and he beats me whenever he loses. That's a lot of the time, almost every day now.

"I'm okay with the girls during the day when he isn't home. We play outside, make snowmen, and go sledding. I like it; we have a good time together. But toward the end of the day when he's due home, I start getting all uptight. I start yelling at the kids and hitting them. It's nothing *they* do; it's *me*. I get so upset about how it's going to be that I make it awful for them, too. They're getting afraid of me, and I'm afraid of me, too.

"My brother was the one person I could have talked to, but he was killed in a motorcycle accident six months ago. Do you know this is the first time I've ever said that? There hasn't even been anyone for me to tell about my brother, my favorite brother who died." Susan's loneliness had catapulted her into abuse. Although her childhood had been relatively secure and she was a stable person, the combination of the trouble with her husband (which she had been handling for six years with the help of friends when she lived in another city) and the lack of someone to talk to made her a very high risk. If she had had people to support her, she could have reached out for help when she felt her frustration and fear mounting.

We all can help, every one of us. Dickson knows this from his own experience. "I knew a woman who abused her kid," he said. "She lived on the same street we did, right next door in fact. She was kind of the flighty type—hadn't been living there very long. She had just got divorced.

"It was night when we heard her abuse for the first time, and we knew exactly what it was. We could hear the sound of her hitting and then the sound of the kid crying. We knew what it was.

"The next day I saw her on the street, and I tried to talk to her, to be nice to her. She didn't have any friends around there. I said 'hello' to her, but she just looked down at her kid and she said, 'Don't speak to anyone around here. You can't trust anyone.'

"That night we heard the abuse again, and I talked about it with my mom. She's raised seven kids, and she's raised us up pretty good, so I guess she knows something about kids. She said she would go over there the next day and talk to her.

"I don't know exactly what went on, or what Mom said, but I do know my mom took care of that little girl for an hour a day from then on. Mom had the little girl over, and pretty soon her mom started staying for coffee and then for meals, and after a while they were part of our family. We didn't hear those beatings anymore. Like I said, that lady had trouble and needed some help then."

Dickson's mother provided the support the young woman needed to balance some of the stress she was experiencing. She probably accomplished this by talking about ways to handle feelings of anger and resentment the young mother was directing toward her child.

This book was written for people who were abused themselves as children, people who are abusing their children now, people who work with child abusers, and people who care about other people. When we learn to understand the reasons behind child abuse, we may be able to accept abusers, to understand them, and to help them become the kinds of parents they want to be.

One of the questions most often asked by people concerned with the problem of child abuse is, "Can they really change enough? Is there actually hope? Can parents this badly off ever turn into good parents?" The answer seems to be, "Yes, there's *more* than hope." The experiences of our PA members leads us to state clearly that there *is* more than just hope. With the proper opportunity and support, change is a certainty. If we're patient, available, and helpful, change will occur. Situations that used to signal certain disaster will become tolerable and then less frequent.

Parents can learn ways to rechannel aggressive and angry feelings. First, they can find ways of rechanneling, such as punching pillows or cupboards. Then they can find more positive, creative ways, such as scrubbing steps, dancing, or gouging dandelions out of the lawn.

Not only can abusive parents learn to stop behaving negatively toward their children, but they can also continue in their learning process to substitute positive responses for the negative ones. In many cases, this substitution of positive parenting for the negative parenting is as difficult as the cessation of abuse itself. Most of these parents have no positive role models, no memory banks of good parent/child experiences. Each and every positive interaction is a totally new discovery. Finding alternatives is hard work.

Changes usually occur first in the individual's parenting style and then spread out to many other areas. Rosemary's husband has joined a PA group himself so that he can learn to behave in better ways both toward his children and toward his wife. He liked what he saw of her experience, and he feels he needs that help, too. Kandy has migraine headaches once or twice a year now instead of once or twice a week. Bob's little boy is no longer a problem in school; his behavior is positive and productive most of the time. Kathy has begun to cry again, and can express her feelings without alcohol for the first time ever. Anna's husband is speaking to his mother-in-law again for the first time in ten years, though he doesn't exactly enjoy it yet. Mary, who used to blush when speaking to a group of three people, now easily addresses audiences numbering in the hundreds. Vicky, who threw up the first time she was interviewed, now appears on national television without a tremor. Parents who used to be terrified to be alone with their children for fear of hitting them, now enjoy caring for them. Children who wouldn't speak at all have learned to speak and play well with other children. It was during a radio interview that Michael explicitly summed up his change. "Now I have learned when I'm upset to put my fist into some THING instead of into some ONE, and it's a lot better for our family now."

So, yes, there is more than a hope. Change isn't easy; it isn't always pleasant; it doesn't always feel very good as it begins. But there *is* a pot of gold at the end of the rainbow following this storm.

Chris Herbruck is partner and co-founder of the Creative Communication Center in Cleveland, Ohio, and coordinator of Parents Anonymous of Northeastern Ohio, Inc. She travels extensively in the Ohio area, giving general and technical in-service presentations to parents, professionals, and general audiences.